TEN ETERNAL QUESTIONS

TEN ETERNAL QUESTIONS

WISDOM, INSIGHT, AND REFLECTION FOR LIFE'S JOURNEY

By Zoë Sallis

CHRONICLE BOOKS
SAN FRANCISCO

First published in the United States in 2006 by Chronicle Books LLC.

Library of Congress Cataloging-in-Publication Data

Sallis, Zoë.
Ten eternal questions : wisdom, insight, and reflection for life's journey/ by Zoë Sallis.
p. cm.
ISBN-13: 978-0-8118-5367-5
ISBN-10: 0-8118-5367-5
1. Spiritual life—Miscellanea. 2. Conduct of life—Miscellanea.
3. Celebrities—Interviews. I. Title.
BL624.S223 2005
100--dc22
2005023360

Manufactured in China.

Distributed in Canada by Raincoast Books
9050 Shaughnessy Street
Vancouver, British Columbia V6P 6E5

10 9 8 7 6 5 4 3 2 1

Chronicle Books LLC
85 Second Street
San Francisco, California 94105

www.chroniclebooks.com

To John and Danny

"... Love is not love
Which alters when it alteration finds,
Or bends with the remover to remove:
O, no! it is an ever-fixèd mark
That looks on tempests and is never
shaken."

WILLIAM SHAKESPEARE

CONTENTS

TO THE GREATEST OF FRIENDS

Speak to Him then for He hears,
and Spirit with Spirit can meet. . .
Closer is He than breathing,
And nearer than hands and feet.

ALFRED, LORD TENNYSON

INTRODUCTION

> The most beautiful experience you can have is a sense of the mysterious. It is the fundamental emotion that stands at the cradle of true art and true science. Whoever does not know it and can no longer wonder, no longer marvel, is as good as dead, and his eyes are dimmed.
>
> ALBERT EINSTEIN

Socrates thought the unexamined life was not worth living. Perhaps that is why he roamed the streets of Athens accosting people and asking them their thoughts and beliefs on a whole range of subjects. But how many people nowadays would agree with Socrates that discussing ideas is the mark of a civilized society? Philosophical and ethical questions often seem to fade from our minds once we have left behind the youthful stage of sitting with friends arguing all night about every topic under the sun.

I used to love doing that. I still do. And it was while my son, Danny, and I were tossing back and forth ideas about life that the idea for this book emerged. It struck me that it might be fascinating to put some fundamental questions to people from different walks of life who were in the public eye yet might never before have been asked to give their views on such subjects.

I began interviewing people for the book around five years ago. It has been a long journey and a great experience. I remember one magical interview sitting on a tree-shaded wooden bench in the foothills of the Pyrenees, the air filled with birdsong. Another in an exquisite apartment in Paris. Others in a museum in Israel, surrounded by sculptures, with waves crashing on the rocks below; in a spiritual center; a mosque in London; in a grand old villa in Cuba; in homes in the Hollywood hills and artists' studios; and on the windswept sands of Los Angeles' Venice Beach. And I will never forget driving in Cape Town to interview Nelson Mandela and seeing his prison, Robben Island, in the distance.

People sometimes find questions about their deepest beliefs quite disconcerting. I can only marvel and be thankful that so many people were willing to respond to that challenge and able to be so extraordinarily encouraging when I turned up to see them. I appreciated the responses of people I had never met before, such as Charles Le Gai Eaton, a writer and authority on Islam, who, in my first rather raw attempt at interviewing, gave me the benefit of his experience, intelligence, and sensitivity. And also all the responses of people I have known for very many years. The only responses included here that are not the result of a personal interview are those from His Holiness the Dalai Lama. I contacted his office, which directed me to relevant passages from his teachings, and then I sought permission from the publishers to include them here.

I thought most people would be interested in the answers to the following ten questions:

1. What is your concept of God?

In the East they often say that God is nearer to us than breathing. Is this sense of natural affinity with a higher power very far from what science is now starting to tell us: that human beings may be programmed to believe in God, and that there could be an evolutionary advantage in having a brain with the capacity to believe in God? Could this belief be a reality, not just a concept?

2. Do you think this life is all there is, or do you believe in an afterlife?

Do we have a soul and does that soul exist after our bodily death? Might there be not only an afterlife but also a whole series of material reincarnations? Or, as some physicists conjecture, is it possible that multiple variations of ourselves exist simultaneously in parallel universes?

3. Do you accept the concept of karma, in the sense of cause and effect?

Isaac Newton, in his third law of motion, describes the principle that for every action there is an equal and opposite reaction. To what extent does the inexorable law of karma, that we reap what we have sown, apply to our conduct in this life, or other lives?

4. What is your moral code, in relation to right and wrong?

Ethics, conscience, guilt, education, spirituality, listening to the still voice within—how do we determine a moral code for ourselves? What guides us, what yardstick can we use when morals change so much from century to century and even from year to year?

5. Do you believe you have a destiny, and do you see yourself as here to fulfill it?

Are our destinies preordained? Do we have only conditioned free will, or do we create our own destiny in the here and now, subject to certain limitations (and capabilities) inherent in some individuals' DNA?

6. What has life taught you so far?

"Life can only be understood backward, but it must be lived forward," said Kierkegaard. Do we begin to understand more about life only as we grow older?

7. What advice or words of wisdom would you like to pass on to those close to you?

Is fear of the Lord the beginning of wisdom, as the Bible tells us? To what extent should we give advice to other people, and will they take it?

8. Do you believe our survival on planet Earth is being threatened?

Is Zac Goldsmith, editor of the *Ecologist* magazine, correct in thinking that without an immediate change in our ways, humankind could disappear very soon? Or are there already positive signs of change and grounds for optimism in our historical ability to adapt and survive?

9. Who do you most admire in this world, historical or living?

Should we judge people by who they are, what they do, or what they aspire to? In our own lifetime, are there people whose characters and achievements rank with those of great men and women of the past?

10. How do you find peace within yourself?

Is inner peace found in solitude, meditation, prayer, music, or the contemplation of nature? Or can it arise from activity, involvement with other people, and creative struggle?

The answers to these questions in the pages that follow are even more varied and intriguing than I expected. The order in which they are given is an entirely personal choice and one that I believe to be both evocative and fluent. The answers are sometimes surprising, moving, deeply committed, or even, on occasion, fresh and funny in their impromptu candor. And they reveal much about the character and personality of all those who were generous enough to spend time with me and share their opinions so frankly. I hope readers will enjoy and value hearing these answers as much as I have.

QUESTION

I

What is your concept of God?

Paulo Coelho

Moses asked God, "Who are you?" He said, "I am." He didn't finish the sentence. So He is the verb, the entity that unifies the subject and the object. It is impossible to give a description of God because every time you try to do that you somehow lose the complexity and, at the same time, the simplicity of Him/Her. I believe in God, not because I have logical reasons to believe but because it was a choice. So my concept is based on my experience of faith in God.

Harry Dean Stanton

God is nondefinable. One word the Taoists have for it is "the nameless." It is not in the sensory realm or the realm of consciousness, ultimately. It's the noumenon—the nothing, the void, and out of that comes the phenomenon, the manifestation of everything. I think every breath is a prayer. Every moment is a prayer and God is everywhere and is all-inclusive. One might call that pantheistic.

"I believe in God, not because I have logical reasons to believe but because it was a choice."

PAULO COELHO

Bono

The idea that there is love and logic behind the universe is something I hold dear. The idea that it should express itself as a child born in shit-and-straw poverty is one that gives me a reason to get out of bed in the morning. It's just mind-blowing to me. I came home once at Christmas, from tour, and I went to St. Patrick's Cathedral to hear the boys' choir sing the carol service. I was tired and I was just doing this as a romantic thing, not really thinking about it as an act of worship or anything. I was given a bad seat behind one of the pillars in this huge hall and I couldn't really hear the words the choir was singing. So, to stop falling asleep, as I hadn't been to bed in days, I concentrated on the sheet in front of me, and it really did dawn on me how perfect it was that this thing we call God would choose to express itself as a child born in a barn, as we say here in Dublin. That's the most striking idea I think we have of God. I think that wherever you look for God you'll still have to pass through that door of humility and that door of complete vulnerability that a child has. There are very few musicians who don't believe in God.

Jools Holland

I think of God partly as a nice big bloke with a beard who oversees everything, and can be seen in the details of everything that is good, like a beautiful chord change, or an act of kindness to a stranger, or a proportion of a building that's beautiful, or an umbrella that keeps somebody dry. Somebody who is bigger and more important than the rest of us.

Zac Goldsmith

Every language, every culture has its own word or words for God. And even between the polar opposite religions like Buddhism and Islam, there are overriding similarities in the understanding of this term. In a sense, God is something bigger than us. He is beyond our understanding. If nothing else, He should inspire deference and humility. For me, the living world, the planet, is a miracle of God. It is of a beauty that cannot be re-created or improved. It is, as virtually every traditional religion accepts, a gift, and we should treat it as such. God is the name given to that which we cannot understand, despite the arrogance of modern science and technology. It is a mystery that should remain a mystery. Attempting to unravel that mystery, as our government-backed geneticists are doing, will trigger uncontrollable repercussions. God, for me, is everything. As is said in the Qur'an, "In every leaf, in every shadow lies the image of God." The Earth itself is, in a sense, the reflection of God.

"As is said in the Qur'an, 'In every leaf, in every shadow lies the image of God.'"

ZAC GOLDSMITH

Shimon Peres

Even when in doubt don't cut Him out! Since we cannot explain things logically in a Cartesian manner and the creation of life is still a great mystery, the way we are being managed and the way order is being kept, we need a God in order to fill the lulls, the holes in our concept. Also we need a Lord inside ourselves because without a Lord we could become animals. So we need Him outside ourselves in order to explain what happened and what is happening, and we need Him in ourselves in order to have a conscience, in order to have values. Basically I agree with Flaubert who said that there is a division between Lord and man, in that the Lord is responsible for the beginning and the end and we are responsible for everything in between. This makes life easier.

There is a difference between religion and faith. Religion is an organization, a hierarchy, an order. Faith is something you carry in your heart and there is no intermediary between the Lord and yourself. No hierarchy, no orders—so from that point of view I am not religious. I don't believe I need anybody between the Lord and myself. I need Him in myself; I don't need an intermediary.

Dadi Janki with Sister Jayanti

God, the parent of all human souls, is the Father and creator of the universe. There is a great deal of confusion in the world about Him. But for myself there is a very clear connection and a feeling of close relationship. God is subtle, complete, and forever the bestower, the benefactor of all. The one who doesn't have any discrimination against anyone. We see God as a being of light, and within the light there are all the virtues and powers, and so love, truth, peace, joy, and wisdom. God is the reservoir of these qualities, which is why we are able to experience all the levels of connections with God as mother, father, teacher, friend, beloved Satguru, and guide.

Albina du Boisrouvray

Einstein taught us that everything is energy, so I suppose God has to do with strength and the energy of love and light, positive things and goodness. He is not the deity personified by religions.

Alfredo Guevara

God exists in the deepest part of your own conscience. Daily life and the constant babble that surrounds it and us—the babble that can be more than mere noise but the whole pressure of existence and the need to survive; in other words, the rhythm of modern man, of modern life—is not conducive to looking into oneself.

I think that modern man, the people of our times, need silence and reflection and have renounced these things almost without realizing it, and by renouncing silence and reflection, people are fundamentally renouncing their own humanity and maybe, if he exists, renouncing God himself. The Catholic Church and, I suppose, other churches and religions too, preach the need for this turning into oneself, for pause, for reflection . . . to regularly take time out from the march. Usually people choose the loneliest places, where there appears to be the least company. But they are seeking the company of the universe. This communion with the universe, this internal-external vision of the immensity, the limitless immensity of the infinite, is my relationship with God. There is something like an invisible presence of the very essence of harmony. A sort of musical resonance.

For the Greek philosophers, the idea of universal harmony as a practical explanation of everything already existed; and this vision and conviction returned during the Renaissance years when they were rediscovered in their purity, and this extremely rich legacy could be addressed within a different framework. In studying Einstein, I've come to realize that his most brilliant intuitions, the most effective directions, were governed by the idea of universal harmony. I would say that this is the path a thinking person should take. I live with uncertainty, but uncertainty does not crush me. Hope is always open to mankind.

Michael Fitzpatrick

The divine presence is expressed most directly for me through music. It is one thing for me to listen to it, but it is another thing entirely for me to play it, to experience a direct "revelation" of God "within me." This is such a glorious experience. There is a "knowing" that is union with God. The mind is suffused in light. It is a very mystical experience. My heart is open and full. Love fills my entire being. I hear it turn into sound.

Jilly Cooper

My concept of God was determined by my grandmother, who said that you were a grain of sand in a jam jar and God was the water all around you, all the time. Despite the dreadful things that happen in the world, I believe God is a benign presence. You can't look at a wildflower or a butterfly without thinking some divine being must have created it.

Richard Dawkins

My concept of God is that it is a human-made construct. It is possible that there are beings in the universe so much greater than us that we would think of them as gods were we ever to meet them. But if we ever do discover them, it will turn out that they have evolved by the same kind of gradual process as we have. So gods are not beings that create universes, or influence human lives, or listen to human prayers, or forgive human sins, etc. There is nothing supernatural. If there are beings superior to us, then they are natural beings who have evolved on other planets by the same process. In other words, they are not gods at all. So there is no such thing as a God except in the human imagination.

"There is no such thing as a God except in the human imagination."

RICHARD DAWKINS

Una M. Kroll

God is Love, but God is also unknowable, beyond all passions, imaginations, and experience. Yet God can be dimly apprehended through the expression of Love in creation, and the response of human beings to love of God incarnate in the person of Jesus Christ. As a Christian I search for union with God, who is always beyond any anthropomorphic image I may construct of God, through following the teachings of Jesus and through waiting on the guidance of the Holy Spirit who, I believe, will "lead me into all truth" (John 14).

Nelson Mandela

The question of God is a private matter, between the supernatural entity that you believe in and yourself. All that I am prepared to say is that religion, whether it is Christian or Hindu or Muslim, is the most powerful force in the world. Whether you are religious or not, if you don't take that into account you will make serious mistakes.

"Religion, whether it is Christian or Hindu or Muslim, is the most powerful force in the world."

NELSON MANDELA

Jack Nicholson

I don't have a concept of God, although I have a lot of thoughts about it. I more or less have a space for what I don't know, and a very human superstitious belief in the wisdom of nature. I envy people of faith. I am not a very faith-oriented person, and anything that touches on it seems to be outside my understanding. I do pray. I find myself talking to things in the top of my head a lot: if-anyone-is-listening sort of mode. What really is essential to us all is fear of death or the unknown.

Farah Pahlavi

God for me is a guide, a teacher, a friend, and a protector. He shows the path to everything that is good and beautiful. He is always present, He is merciful, and He is there to help you in the difficult times of your life. He is the only one who completely knows what is within you.

Seyyed Hossein Nasr

God is absolute; absolute in the metaphysical sense that He excludes all that is other than Him. He is totally Himself, the absolute Reality, that which alone is. Then God is infinite; infinite in the sense that He contains all possibilities within His infinite nature. There is nothing in the universe, nothing that has been, nothing that is or nothing that will be in the whole of the universe, in the whole of the cosmos, in the whole of the creation, which does not have its roots in the Divine Reality. He is also the source of all goodness and, since it is in the nature of the good to give of itself, from this Divine Goodness flows all that exists—that is, the universe in its vastest sense. For example, I do not "think" of God as being only transcendent, nor as being only immanent. God is at once both transcendent and immanent. He is beyond all that we can conceive of Him and yet He is at the center of our hearts and in the heart of all of His creation.

I am not one of those who claim that theology is not important, that only "spirituality" counts. Theology is extremely important; theology is there to prevent these concepts of God from becoming distorted in our mind, from our entertaining wrong concepts. Ultimately, however, the goal of religion is not only to provide us with the right concepts; it is to enable us to experience the spiritual life. I believe that the ultimate goal of the human being is to bear witness to the Divine Reality in this world and to know and experience the Divine Reality within oneself. I think that the ultimate goal of all religions is that knowing and experiencing of the Divine.

Emma Sergeant

I can't imagine what it is like not to believe in God. It must be an empty, colorless, humorless world. I pray and I believe in God, that He is everywhere and in everything. I feel at the end of every working day like thanking God because I don't believe it's me who has done the work, I believe I just put out my hands. Any creative endeavor is thanks to my God.

David Frost

My concept of God is as a force that we can tap into. It is difficult to say if God can respond to any specific requests, because that involves Him in so much that is wrong in the world, as well as what is right. You have to come back to the original concept, that man chose to reject God and therefore that this world's ills and evils are not God's responsibility but God is still there and available to help those who believe in Him, and who can tap into His power. In that way I think one has a coherent structure. Yes, I do believe in God.

His Holiness The Dalai Lama

Buddhism is atheistic in the sense that a creator God is not accepted; rather Buddhism presents a view of self-creation, that one's own actions create one's life situations. In this light, it has been said that Buddhism is not a religion, but a science of the mind.

Michael Radford

There is a concept that you historically live with, which is of a large man with a beard, who looks after you, punishes you, makes you want to do good things. I was brought up that way, even though my mother was Jewish. I was brought up in a Christian, middle-class Anglican way. So you never really get rid of that sense of "something there." But I have no concept of God in a proper biblical sense. I often wish that I understood or had some sort of experience of God because it would make life much easier for me. I am one of those people who are condemned to live in doubt. What controls my moral dignity, my morality, and everything is a mixture of a sense that there is an ultimate goodness somewhere and there is something to that old bearded man sitting in the sky that I learned about when I was a kid. I have this problem with God, because I think God is just a part of the route to understanding the spiritual nature of the universe in very different terms.

Anjelica Huston

I see God as being in all things. I think everything on Earth is an analogy of God. Just as the body contains all the elements, we are all the elements that are God. I would say that in everything—in instinct, feeling, emotion, love—all these things correspond to God as much as material things, such as air, earth, leaves, snowflakes.

Bob Geldof

I don't have a concept of God, so it follows that there is no belief. It strikes me as being an odd idea, and I am not trying to be smart by saying that it is all a bit "Star Trekkie," you know, the supreme being, or being a speck of intelligence in the great cosmos, or a ray of light, or a guy with a beard, or a woman. I don't get it. It strikes me as weird. Why would there have to be one?

"God is pure love in its most supreme form."

STEVE VAI

Steve Vai

I believe that God in his fullest is virtually beyond our ability to conceptualize with the human senses that we have. But there will be a time in all of our existences when we will be able to experience God. Our relationship with Him is individual and personal and constantly evolving. I use "Him" but that's just for convenience. I don't think God is a Him or Her or any of those things that are identifiable. I like to think that God is pure love in its most supreme form. Much human love is selfish but divine love is something different. I believe we all experience elements of God every day but may not be aware.

Peter Ustinov

We cannot be held responsible for all the fantastic things around us. Therefore we must, for our own sakes, create something bigger than ourselves in order to discipline ourselves. But apart from that I have no idea what it is or who it is. All I know is that I once wrote that a twinge of conscience is a glimpse of God. I don't believe in anything particular, but I am willing to be surprised at any moment. It is that quality which I think is also the link to anything spiritual and divine.

Frei Betto

God is love. He who loves knows God, says St. John in his first letter. It is interesting to note that he does not say, "He who knows loves God . . ." The reason is that every experience of love is an experience of God, even if the person is not conscious of it. Personally, I see Jesus as the revelation of God in the history of mankind. God dwells in every heart.

Ed Begley Jr.

I believe in a power greater than myself, some common force in the universe that unites it. It's what has given us the miracle of the Big Bang and the miracle of DNA. I have very limited knowledge of scientific matters, but I do know that in the genetic code the same four nucleic acid bases arranged in triplets specify the order of the same 20 amino acids found in the proteins of every living thing. That's a unifying force, it's part of the mystery of the universe. The more I learn about science, the more I believe in God. So yes, I have a great deal of belief.

Gianfranco Ferre

God is something like a mind that has been able to project everything and make it work, someone that sometimes gives us signs for what we have to believe. Yes, I believe in a certain God.

Sophia Loren

For me, the concept of God is not something that can be explained in terms of reason and rationality.

Robert Fisk

Clearly this didn't all happen because nine billion years ago two gas clouds bumped together. I always have this conversation with my driver in Beirut, I point out to him that if you are traveling over the mountains of Lebanon and you see the trees and the dark blue sky and the snow, and we talk to each other in the language of angels, we human beings, it wasn't gas clouds—there was something, which obviously was a power that we don't understand. I have no idea, I am not a believer.

"I don't think I would still be alive without prayer. It is only God who protected me."

MANGOSUTHU BUTHELEZI

Mangosuthu Buthelezi

I absolutely believe in God. Yes, I pray. In fact, when I look at the journeys I have traveled and the enemies I have had and the efforts that have been made to kill me, I don't think I would still be alive without prayer. It is only God who protected me. Zulu people have a word for God, Umvelingangi, meaning the one who appeared first, the Creator. I was brought up a Christian, and my concept of God is that of a Christian. I cannot face the day without a little time for meditation in the morning.

Ilana Goor

I'm not a great believer in God. I believe in myself because I have not seen any hand coming from anywhere helping the people who don't help themselves. Obviously there is some power, but I don't know how to describe it, I don't know anybody who has seen it. I think the most important thing is believing in what you are aiming for. So I guess this is my God, believing in the things that I am going after. I do not pray or meditate; I believe in myself.

Robert Graham

I believe in God, but I don't have a concept of divinity. I pray by working, so I think that the work is a prayer. You pray by working; you pray that you can make work that's got a certain amount of authenticity. Artists are lucky to have such a direct connection to spirituality. Most people don't; most people need to have a structure to allow them to enter into it.

Charles Le Gai Eaton

God is beyond all concepts. If I must seek a definition, then: the "face" or aspect that the one and only Reality turns toward humankind, so that the inaccessible becomes accessible. There is an inspired saying of Muhammad (in which God speaks through him): "I was a Hidden Treasure and I loved to be known, so I created the worlds." A kind of reciprocity is possible because the innermost depths of the human creature contain, as it were, a reflection of the "Hidden Treasure" in the "mirror of the heart."

Gore Vidal

I have no notion of an anthropomorphic God (God in man's image), nor the idea that there would be anything remotely human or understandable at the center of the cosmos, as it sounds vain.

QUESTION

2

Do you think this life is all there is, or do you believe in an afterlife?

I have the approach of Pascal, the French philosopher who said it made more sense to bet on something than on nothing. If I just go by my logic, I don't see anything after this life. I see people when they die, and I see death. On the other hand, I *feel* there is something. I feel a connection with people who are not here anymore, and a connection to what we call God, in terms of light and love. If the world has any purpose, then that means there is a God, something spiritual beyond us; transcendental spirituality I can call it; something after this passage.

I feel that we are on a trip, we are going somewhere, but I have given up trying to comprehend or discover it. I just put myself in the hands of that power, or that light, and I try to float and let myself be taken and give up the control to go wherever we are going. Scientifically and physically the material world is so precise, so coldly, minutely precise, that there has to be a plan, whether tiny or large, in the cosmos. It is incredible. It cannot be chance or necessity. I feel the absurdity of nothingness proves there is something.

"I feel the absurdity of nothingness proves there is something."

ALBINA DU BOISROUVRAY

Gianfranco Ferre

For me, the afterlife is not a physical life. Depending on how much we love the people that passed away, we can make them continue to love us and live with us because we can have a certain kind of energy that is created by the love that we had with them. When they die, that is it. It is your memory of them, the intense relationship that you have with them that makes them "live" in your mind.

Alfredo Guevara

It was only when man was capable of dissecting a corpse and knowing the whole internal mechanism and its interrelationships that we began to understand that there is a system which makes it work, which makes the interrelation of the parts determine the whole. In human beings could this system be the soul? I don't know. But whether or not it is the soul, I know that the system cannot perish. It doesn't die, because nothing dies, everything remains. I don't know how, but that which exists, exists.

On Earth it has existed since the beginning of history, from the beginning of memory, whether it be the memory of a society or the memory of those who loved that which existed. Because everything that exists, exists not only in itself, it exists also in others. And all those I have loved exist in me, carry on existing in me. I suppose that I will continue to exist in those who have loved me and in the works I have made. If I have sown anything, it is surely not because I imparted a true or reasonable thought but also because I have been loved because of those ideas or because I put so much love into them. I cannot accept nothingness. Intellectually, I cannot accept it.

Michael Fitzpatrick

I think this *is* the afterlife! No, seriously, it seems to me, based on that feeling that comes over me when I'm playing music, that we can be in the eternal here and now, and when we're in it we realize that it's all birth and death and renewal, like the seasons, like the turning of the universe. We are notes in the music of the universe. The music plays us forever.

"We are notes in the music of the universe. The music plays us forever."

MICHAEL FITZPATRICK

His Holiness The Dalai Lama

I am a Buddhist. I believe that a human being may take on the form of a lower being. Where you are born in the next life is not dependent on your present body. This is dependent on unwholesome activities and virtue. The basic thing is our own karmic force. That is the seed. The seed alone, however, is not sufficient; it must interact with water and soil. So, similarly, you have to think not only in terms of cause but also in terms of conditions. Basically it is very clear. The main material of our physical body comes from parents. But our mind, our self, does not.

Dadi Janki with Sister Jayanti

All the traditions have said that the soul is eternal and the difference is that some will say that there is an afterlife, which is somewhere else or in another dimension, some will say there is another birth here in this physical, material place. I believe that I, the soul, am on a physical journey, and this particular physical body is a costume, but when I have completed the role that I have to play with this costume, there is death. After the departure of the soul from this body there is another birth and so I believe there is some continuity in terms of life here on Earth, a number of births and rebirths. Yes, I do believe in reincarnation, but we use the word rebirth rather than reincarnation. Reincarnation implies that the soul is coming from another dimension to this physical place and once it is here it takes rebirth here.

Gore Vidal

We are nothing more than a race of bacteria which has infested the Earth and is devouring it and destroying it and soon we will be gone. The idea that our ghosts will go on into all eternity is nonsense, except the fact that we are recorded on light. All light will have our images on it, apparently, until the end of the galaxy or cosmos. So, in a way, there is immortality like old movies, or

TV, which is total immortality, because they keep replaying it all the time. So we may be on a tape being replayed all the time, but when we are dead, we are gone.

Farah Pahlavi

I believe that your afterlife depends on your deeds in this life. In the end people remember you for your deeds, whether good or bad, and for me that defines heaven or hell. Good deeds are not forgotten, even after thousands of years, because they reveal the way to those who come after us.

Seyyed Hossein Nasr

We have a preterrestrial, pretemporal, prehistorical reality in God. Then we have the second phase of our existence, which is in this world, and finally we will have the journey back to God. To be human is to be in a sense condemned to immortality. There is no way of evading immortality. There are some people who think that they can live a life in the forgetfulness of God and when death comes our life and consciousness are just finished. That, however, is not the case. The paradises, hells, and purgatorial states are real. Almost all religions, not only the Abrahamic but also Zoroastrianism, Buddhism, and Hinduism, speak about both the infernal and paradisal states: they are real. Some religions, such as Confucianism, do not speak explicitly and in detail about the posthuman states; but they do not, however, in any way deny them. Our soul does not die with our bodily death.

The simple extinction of the soul with earthly death would be too easy a way out. Whatever we do, we do as human beings; we are responsible for our actions, which have consequences for us beyond the life of this world. In being human, we are given the opportunity through our "God-likeness," or being His *khalifah,* or representative here on Earth, to remember God in this world: either to live the good life, and therefore after death to be in proximity of God, the source of all beauty and goodness; or to live a life which is not based on goodness. After death we realize what goodness is, and that the very separation from the source of all goodness is hell. Yes, I definitely believe that the individual soul with all of its faculties, not only the rational and intellectual faculties but also the faculty of imagination, survives death.

"There is no way of evading immortality."

SEYYED HOSSEIN NASR

Jack Nicholson

I act as though this is all there is; this is what my so-called sense tells me. Of course I hope for the continuance of what has been.

Jilly Cooper

I based a story in one of my novels on the experience of a friend who was declared clinically dead during a caesarean. All she was conscious of was going down a dark tunnel with a wonderful white light at the end, and all she wanted to do was go through it to reach this unbelievable happiness. But at the door was an angel with a clipboard who said, "You can't come through, we are not ready for you and there are people on Earth who need you." She was desolate because she wanted to get through the dazzling white lights so badly. When she finally came around, she found that her baby was alive and her husband was obviously desperate for her to live too. I think it's a very moving story. I think that is what the other side must be like. I don't believe that this life is all there is, and I do believe in the afterlife.

Una M. Kroll

Jesus said to Thomas his apostle, who would not believe until he had proof of Jesus' resurrection: "Blessed are those who have not seen and yet have come to believe" (John 20:29). I believe in an afterlife in that dark unknowing way which I call faith. I believe that my body and mind will die properly and that consciousness as I know it now will die, but that I will be reborn in a new way into the love of God. That Love will not absorb me but enfold me, preserving my individuality as a child of God, yet leading me into an encounter with the very essence of Love.

"I believe in an afterlife in that dark unknowing way which I call faith."

UNA M. KROLL

STEVE VAI

It is my belief (and actually many peoples' belief) that the soul is eternal and that it moves from body to body through the concept of reincarnation. It enters the world with a specific body, set of moral values, and destination that are designed to help evolve the soul to the point of purging it of desires by separating it from the mind. This aids the soul in its eventual ascent into a state of God-consciousness. As for an afterlife, when we die and are in the interim state of an afterlife, it is an endless world with fathomless levels. According to our karmas generated in the previous life (or past lives), for a time we dwell in this afterlife abyss of thought-forms. Some karmas may be good and some bad but elements of them can be worked out in the myriad heavens and hells that exist in the afterlife. This experience helps shape the moral fiber of the soul, thus giving us the tools to deal with what lies ahead in our next life. This concept is something that I have felt since early childhood. Obviously I can't prove this, but I do believe that there are people walking on the planet who have firsthand experience and knowledge of these things.

Sharon Stone

I believe in Einstein's theory of time, that all our lives are happening at the same time.

Shimon Peres

I think life is what it is. It is an occasion for creatures, for people, to taste life, to contribute what they can and then in another way to disappear. I think life is being continued anyway so I don't have to think that my ego is going to repeat itself endlessly, but I am not the end of anything and life will be continued without me. That will be the continuation of all of us, it's not personal. Reincarnation? I think it's a mistake because then you postpone your good things for after death and I think you have to use them right away!

Richard Dawkins

I am absolutely confident that there is no afterlife—in other words, a prolongation of the individual consciousness. If you redefine afterlife in other ways, then genes do in a sense go on from body to body, but I think it would be misleading to use the word afterlife for that.

Sophia Loren

I do think that after this life we must expect something that rewards our good behavior as well as something that punishes our sins.

Charles Le Gai Eaton

I could not call myself a Muslim if I did not believe in the Hereafter (the "real life," according to the Qur'an). But what does "belief" mean? Each of us is a city of many factions, often opposed to each other. A significant story: an Irish priest was asked what his parishioners believed about the afterlife. He said, "They believe all that the Church teaches about Judgment, Heaven, and Hell. At the same time, they believe that when you're dead that's it." Two beliefs side by side!

Few, if any of us, are consistent, single-minded. If someone believes without any shadow of doubt that Paradise exists and that he is fit for it, then he must look forward to death with eager anticipation and his whole life passes in the radiance of this certainty. Of how many people is this true, even among fervent "believers"? If you ask me, "Do you believe?" I must answer, "Yes!" If you ask, "Are you sure?" I turn away; or else I reply, "Sometimes, in prayer, in invocation." If you were to ask me on a cold, wet morning when I am out of sorts, you might get a different answer.

Harry Dean Stanton

Afterlife? Well, where were you before you were born? No, I do not believe in an individual soul or persona, or an individual entity. That's not scientifically accurate and it is obvious, you know, that we are made up of just energy. We are vibrations of energy, that's all it is. We are made up of atoms and it is all transient, nothing's solid. It's very obvious that we are all going to go—the planet is going to go, the sun is going to go, and one time it wasn't here. These are all scientifically proven facts.

Paulo Coelho

I do not believe in time, therefore I cannot believe in something after or before. I believe we are living here and now, in the moment; the universe is being created and being destroyed in the present tense. I am convinced that everything is happening at the same time, in the same point all over the universe. So here I am talking to you but at the same time living a life that happened ten thousand years ago and a life that will happen ten thousand years later. That is why I believe that everything that I do here now can redeem me from my past. Time is an abstraction, something we use to get some references, basically memory.

"I believe we are living here and now, in the moment; the universe is being created and being destroyed in the present tense."

PAULO COELHO

Nelson Mandela

Some people believe there is another world when you die. Others say the world is what we know. These questions are actually private.

Mangosuthu Buthelezi

In Zulu society in ancient times, before being exposed to the Christian Gospel, we believed in the hereafter—to the extent that when a person was buried, he was buried with some of his things, utensils and so on, symbolically indicating that even after death there is life. It goes much further in the Zulu religion. Zulus have always believed in the ancestral spirits interceding between themselves and God. The Zulus have also in their culture a ceremony after the death of someone important. It's a cleansing ceremony called "Ihlambo," in which the dead person is invited home to look after his family.

Bono

I'll be very disappointed if this is all there is. I'm having such a great life. I'm never surprised at the ugliness in the world, nor by the beauty of it. I understand the survival of the fittest, but people who have a lot less fun still glean from their lives the precious stones of friendship, insight, and knowledge that they will take with them forever, no matter what their circumstances. I do think they are the eternal things. I love the idea of hell as a flame that will burn away all the crap and only the precious stones will remain. I think that's probably where things get evened out and I think that's probably what that idea of "the first will be last" means, that if you have spent your whole life accumulating material things and material ideas about yourself, you will be left with very little. I feel I have a lot of faith. Musicians tend to have a lot of faith. When you hear one note in your head you have to have faith that there's another one round the corner. If my first life is going to be the last, I'm probably in trouble.

Robert Graham

I don't know. It's a mystery, but you do live on through your work, so that's another chance of having immortality in that sense.

Frei Betto

There is something after, as there is life outside the uterus—unimaginable for the baby. As Dostoyevsky suggested, even if Christ were to be proved untrue, I would still stick to Christ. Christ assured us that after this life we enter eternal life, that is, the ineffable sphere of love, or, as Brazilian natives put it, the Land of No Evil.

Zac Goldsmith

In a way I wish I had been raised faithfully to one of the great religions. That way I would know—or at least believe that I know—the answer. As it is, I believe that life, in every form, is something that cannot be truly destroyed. What happens to all that energy, all those tangles of feelings, thoughts, memories, and emotions, I don't know. I worry, though, that in today's world, where religion has become something of an abstract tag-on formality with little significance to everyday living, that belief in the afterlife is an unjustified comfort. When we are destroying this planet, believing that this Earth is a stepping-stone to a distant celestial city is a very convenient means of avoiding responsibility for what we are doing.

David Frost

Obviously no one knows the answer to that question, but I would say that I believe there is an afterlife, that in some way the spiritual development that you have had during your life lives on in some way that we can only guess at. I do believe there is something.

Ilana Goor

Unfortunately, I believe in life right now. That's why I am always scared that time is not enough and the older you get, time becomes shorter. That's the one time that I'm envious of the people who believe that there's another life, because then I feel they have something to look forward to, but I really believe in now, that I have to do it now. I don't believe in reincarnation and all those things because I grew up by myself. I could not go to school because I am dyslexic and I worked very hard for everything I have. I never got any gifts from anybody. So that's the way I am, no gifts.

Emma Sergeant

I believe, strangely enough, in what I think they call the eleventh dimension: I believe that we are here now and that there are parts of us all over the universe. I think that one of the problems today is that there are too many bodies and not enough souls, thanks to medical science. This is my own personal belief. I think that a soul has enormous resonance and therefore why shouldn't it be living a life here, or 100 years ago, or somewhere across in another universe, all at the same time. Maybe we operate like jellyfish, there are bits of us floating around all over the place, having separate existences yet somehow coming back to one nucleus, and the nucleus is the soul.

Jools Holland

Well, I've got a lot of friends who believe in reincarnation. The idea that you keep coming back, personally, rather depresses me. So the answer is, like everyone else, I don't know, except that probably the human spirit does go on to somewhere better.

Peter Ustinov

We believe in eternity out of fear that all this acquisition of knowledge is there for no reason at all. It seems a terrible waste. At the same time I am just as terrified by the idea of immortality: where does it lead to? I think in order to understand a life you have to have a beginning and an end. Death seems to me to be an unfrightening prospect and whether life is eternal or not I neither know nor really care that much.

"We believe in eternity out of fear that all this acquisition of knowledge is there for no reason at all."

PETER USTINOV

David Lynch

I think that life is a continuum. Going to sleep at night and then waking up the next day seems to be a kind of indication of something that could happen—that you live a life, the body dies, and then you keep going again until you graduate. In another whole ballgame.

Michael Radford

I don't believe in an afterlife. I can't possibly see how, rationally, there can be one, I simply don't. I think it's an act of selfishness to believe that somehow or another we continue to exist in some kind of way. We have no consciousness of what happened before we were here. I believe that we depart into that realm of blackness as if we never had been and the only trace of our existence is what is here. It is terrifying, and I feel cold shivers when I think about it, because I am terrified of death. It's an emotional, egotistical cry, "I want to continue to live, I want to continue to be."

Anjelica Huston

I believe if there is another life it is outside of this life. I am always on the lookout for clues, but so far I can't say that I have been given a miraculous insight into the other life.

"This is it. No afterlife, thank God."

BOB GELDOF

QUESTION

3

Do you accept the concept of karma, in the sense of cause and effect?

The word "karma" of course comes from Sanskrit and is related in its meaning to the word "action". In the deeper sense it means that for every action there is a reaction. The law of Newton is, in a sense, the physical application of this universal law. In the moral realm, consequences do not always come back to us immediately. You can do evil to somebody and say that you have gotten away with it, but the consequences boomerang back upon you. In India today, popular Hinduism believes that individual souls are reincarnated in this world on the basis of their karma. This is a view that Islam, Christianity, and Judaism deny, and I have spoken to many great Hindu sages who believe that this modern concept of karma is only a popular belief. It is actually the divine self or *atman* that is reincarnated. The individual soul journeys from one world to another and does not return to the same state of being.

Many Islamic thinkers, such as Ibn 'Arabi and Mulla Sadra, one a Sufi and the other a philosopher, have stated that after death we are born into intermediate worlds according to what we have done and how we have lived in this world, and we continue our journey through these other worlds. If we have not lived a good life, there is no certainty that we will still be born into a central state corresponding to the human state here on Earth. However, there is also always the possibility of forgiveness through repentance, contrition, turning back to God. In Arabic the word for repentance, *tawbah*, means "to turn around." That is one of the remarkable possibilities in the condition of being human. So, although there is without doubt this unbreakable karmic chain on its own level, I believe that it is possible to transcend it. On the highest level it is possible to transcend the karmic chain through divine knowledge, and through faith in, and love of, God.

Una M. Kroll

My understanding of karma is that it is destiny: that destiny depends to some extent upon one's actions in this life. Nevertheless, Christians believe that they are justified by faith, and that faith is a pure gift from God which one cannot earn by meritorious works (see Romans 3). Faith normally issues in good works. It is my firm belief that we are called ultimately to union with God.

"Doing good eventually brings you closer to feeling good."

ANJELICA HUSTON

Anjelica Huston

I believe that karma works itself out in this life on this Earth, and that doing good eventually brings you closer to feeling good. The conscious effort to push yourself outside your normal parameters, or your normal instincts, can sometimes have a deep spiritual effect. Part of my karmic responsibility, I feel, is to be aware of the possibility of going in other directions than the ones I would easily fall back on, such as laziness, or maybe some baser instinct. The idea of wanting to overcome that is my vision of karma.

Charles Le Gai Eaton

A Muslim could never, of course, use or accept the term "karma," but we certainly believe in the chain of cause and effect. This can, however, be broken by the Divine Mercy, hence the Name Al-'Afu, "the Effacer," in the Qur'an—He who effaces sins as though they had never been. Surely in Hindu doctrine, karma is still situated in the realm of *maya*? And the man or woman who is liberated-in-life (the *jivanmukti*) is free from the bonds of *maya*. Classical Islamic theology says that God re-creates creation in every moment. He is not obliged to make the next moment (the next frame in the film) follow on from the previous one as its "effect." He can always break the sequence.

His Holiness The Dalai Lama

As Buddhists, we believe in the law of karma, the natural law of cause and effect. Whatever external causal conditions someone comes across in subsequent lives result from the accumulation of that individual's actions in previous lives. When the karmic force of past deeds reaches maturity, a person experiences pleasurable and unpleasurable mental states. They are but a natural consequence of his own previous actions.

Alfredo Guevara

Yes, I think we pay for the consequences of our actions. But I don't like the idea that there is some charge to be levied. If I am able to perform noble or worthy actions, if I am able to enter someone else's skin to understand them and accept them, for whoever understands accepts, I am a better person. That is my reward. I create it myself. If I cause harm, if I am so selfish that I am unable to understand other people, if I am not able to put myself in their skin and understand their way of being and their vision of the world, I impoverish myself so much, I am such a valueless thing, that that is my punishment, to be a fool, an empty being, to be without love. To translate it into the words of Catholic Christendom, heaven and hell lie within oneself. This is my concept of karma because I fully believe in free will. One is a god, a small god, vulnerable in the universe because we don't really understand our role in it, but nevertheless a small god and we should act like small gods.

Richard Dawkins

An action that you take will influence later events in your own life? There is only this life.

David Lynch

I definitely believe in karma. What you sow is what you reap, and you are creating your future by every thought, word, and action. Things go out and then they return. You never know when they are going to return. Sometimes good things come back to you, sometimes bad. If we want a better future, we can achieve it by our present actions, thoughts, and words. Things will visit us that we have set in motion in the past, in the past in this life and the past in other lives. You can't do anything without it having repercussions, good or bad.

"What you sow is what you reap, and you are creating your future by every thought, word, and action."

DAVID LYNCH

Michael Radford

Emotionally I believe in karma, you have to, otherwise life is too unfair and cruel. I'm torn between what emotionally I would like to feel and what I rationally can accept. All my childhood I wanted to be famous and what I actually noticed about people who are famous is that all of them have huge egos and most of them are cruel to the people around them, and yet we have come to worship and look up to them. So it seems to me that that's not a very karmic position. It seems to me that you do what you do and you seem to get away with it. I think it's necessary to try and deal with what exists within the world itself. Maybe there is an afterlife, a payback time, but I am not banking on it.

Steve Vai

I am a very strong believer in the entire concept of karma and reincarnation. It makes perfect sense. Cause and effect is proven most substantially in mathematics and science. To me it seems as if the entire creation, including elements that we have not the senses to recognize, is entirely built on the concept of cause and effect. Every day that goes by, this becomes more and more clear to me but, as with most spiritual issues, it's virtually impossible to prove. That's sort of the riddle of existence.

Ed Begley Jr.

I don't know that you need to believe in a hereafter to worry about the consequences of your actions. I think there's heaven and hell both right here on Earth, and a lot of it is to do with your own making. Fate plays a role, certainly, but there are people who against insurmountable odds, in the face of unspeakable conditions, find a measure of serenity in their lives. Then there are people who have everything and are just blindly miserable. If material good fortune made people happy, there would be nothing but happy people living in Bel Air and unhappy people living in the bush, and that's hardly the case.

Bono

I think karma is at the very heart of the universe, but divine grace can intervene. I'm much more interested in grace. You can't escape the effect of your actions. But the idea that people go through several lives and that people are born better off in this life because of what they did in the last life, I think is bollocks. This idea has produced the caste system and a lot of other useless hierarchies.

MICHAEL FITZPATRICK

In music, we don't want any bad notes. The same in our lives, we don't want any bad qualities within ourselves—anger, jealousy, mean-spiritedness. When we behave that way, it seems like the world mirrors that back to us. When we emphasize our good qualities, kindness, compassion, charity to strangers, we get those same attributes radiated back to us. The more positive our "tone," the more harmonious we are, the more we bring joy into the world. It takes practice. But yes, I do think we reap what we sow, I do think that what we put out is what comes back, and sometimes it slaps us back real hard.

"When we emphasize our good qualities, kindness, compassion, charity to strangers, we get those same attributes radiated back to us."

MICHAEL FITZPATRICK

Gore Vidal

The big question with reincarnation—if indeed it were true, and many interesting civilizations from the Hindus to Pythagoreans believed it to be true—is what's the point if you can't remember who you were before? What they are trying to say with reincarnation (though the Hindus are never very clear about this) is that we are all made of primal matter, we all come out of the Big Bang, all the atoms that make up the entire universe (without end probably, without beginning probably) are interchangeable. So an ant and Alexander the Great are made out of the same stuff. But individuality, the spirit of Zoë, goes when Zoë goes. Then Zoë is used to rehabilitate Madonna lilies, which I happen to be looking at across the room.

Sharon Stone

What we do in our lives will in some way come back to us, yes.

Farah Pahlavi

Seeds planted with love will always bloom, thrive, and multiply. I believe karma is your action in life, and also the consequence of your action in this life. As a result of my life experience, I now have come to believe that to a large extent, what happens to you is your own choice. You have to keep some values and remind yourself of those values everyday. For example, meeting you has reinvigorated my beliefs, which one tends to neglect from time to time.

Sophia Loren

I find it hard to express a firm opinion about karma one way or the other. But in its various aspects, the idea of our actions determining our fate fascinates me.

Jack Nicholson

My concept of karma is that it is constant and present. It is a first cousin to existentialism. I mean you are what you do. It's always there, and people of little faith like myself might be more inclined to being slothful except for the idea that everything you do has effects, everything counts. I don't have a belief in reincarnation, in the Eastern sense. But I don't think that I would choose a life for myself that was less than directed at the highest principle. This is a man who doesn't have any idea or concept of evil. I never have been able to get my mind around it. Responsibility and failing, that's something I do understand.

Dadi Janki with Sister Jayanti

The idea of our actions having consequences is the only thing that makes sense. On a physical level you can never say that things are happening just like that, at random. There is always a cause and that leads to a certain effect. Sometimes, when you are seeing the effect, you don't know what the cause might be. As with weather patterns, there might be long-distance connections or it might be a long period of time before you see the connection. But definitely there is linkage of cause and effect, and this applies not only on a physical level but also on an emotional level. For example, if I keep causing you pain there is going to come a time when you say enough is enough, and you may cause pain in return. So the good I have done comes back to give me happiness and the evil that I have done comes back to give me pain.

"The idea of our actions having consequences is the only thing that makes sense."

DADI JANKI WITH SISTER JAYANTI

Jools Holland

I think karma is quite immediate, an instant thing. If people are just being good out of self-interest because they believe they are going on to some better place, then I think that's probably the wrong reason for doing it. We should be doing it even if we were going to hell. As a possibility, I think it's such a gloomy idea, the idea of coming back.

David Frost

I think you could argue that when people have been religious or good or kind, there is an effect that lives on, and so the person who has done more of that will be more advanced in the next life. I believe it's possible for people in the next life to catch up, I suppose, catch up on their spiritual life. When I was talking to Billy Graham, I said I suppose that if your God is a God of love, then in the end He has to let everyone into heaven, because, there may be a period of purgatory first, but in the end if He is a God of love, then He has to let everyone into heaven. Billy smiled and said, "He doesn't have to do anything if He is God." Which I thought was a very good summing up.

Jilly Cooper

I never know about karma. If you do believe in fate and predestination I think it is a bit self-defeating, because you tend not to fight so hard as you do if you feel you can determine your future. I think the only answer is to battle on and face up to disaster and be grateful for all the wonderful things in one's life.

Zac Goldsmith

I believe ultimately that what goes around comes around. Common to a lot of traditional people was a belief that decisions of importance should never be taken without first considering how any such decision would be considered by the ancestors, and how it would affect things for future generations. In the modern world, no such considerations are ever taken into account. That's why we are fast depleting the world's resources, killing the world's diversity, and triggering diseases like cancer, which by the time our descendants are maturing will be epidemic. If it is so that we are reborn following death, then yes, our next lives will be miserable as a result of our conduct today. Many of us will be victims of degenerative disease. Many of us will be badly malformed. Many of us will be dealt impossible card-hands. Our descendants will be the victims essentially of our wrongdoing. This is a near certainty, though there is still time to reverse these trends with merely a sprinkling of political honesty.

Harry Dean Stanton

Sure, there's cause and effect. But reincarnation is just another concept, another projection of the ego. There are probably energies in the pool of the super-consciousness that are all connected, but there is not one single personality that is reborn. To me it is very obvious that you come out of nothing. We are programmed genetically, and by our conditioning after we are born. If you do something bad, you are going to get punished, you are going to suffer for it. There is action and reaction.

Emma Sergeant

I do believe in karma. I think it's important that one doesn't try and take revenge on people, because usually they bring about their own downfall. You've got to send them love, especially if you're frightened of them. You have to imagine that you are sending them lilies and dancing girls and bells and smells. Then you feel you are the stronger person and they will condemn themselves.

"To say that the whole of life is just cause and effect, without accidents or incidents, doesn't make sense."

SHIMON PERES

Shimon Peres

Like anything in life, nothing is perfect. There is room for cause and effect, but to say that the whole of life is just cause and effect, without accidents or incidents, doesn't make sense. Rules and regulations are man-made. They are in response to a given situation, they don't have eternal permanence.

Amos Gitai

I am open to any scenarios. I'm not against the karma scenario, but I cannot say that I adhere to it. If somebody would convince me, then maybe I would be convinced, you know, like anything else. But I am not yet convinced.

Paulo Coelho

I don't accept karma in the linear way. I accept that what I do now is affecting my past but I am not paying something for my past. I am all my past lives and they are happening now. I am talking about parallel universes, something that is happening forever and together. It is a difficult concept to explain. In space physics we are starting to understand that we can travel in time, or condense time. So I am several people now talking to you. I believe everything is happening together.

Frei Betto

No, I do not accept the concept of karma. I accept free will.

Bob Geldof

Things that you do in this life come back in the next? Well, I don't believe in a next life. I find it hard to believe in karma intellectually. I think it works as an idea because I have been subject to it in this life. But then that famous aphorism "No good deed goes unpunished" is also true. The worst thing to do is lend a great friend money. You want to do it, but from then on it colors the relationship, not in your eyes but theirs. They are beholden and no one likes to be beholden. I think there's an element of powerlessness about it. Even if they pay you back, it alters things. If one of your mates is in personal or professional trouble and you help him out, that colors the relationship too because where there was parity in your partnership, then suddenly there is a dependency and it alters them, even if it doesn't affect you. It is not a partnership of equals. If the boot was on the other foot, it would be the same. It is the flip side to karma.

Albina du Boisrouvray

Do we come back in another life? I would think that because life is so short and there is so much unfinished business that it would seem again logical and natural that we do have to come back to finish our business. Maybe we live life elsewhere or on another dimension, or come back here. Who knows?

Mangosuthu Buthelezi

I believe one is accountable to the Creator for our actions on Earth.

QUESTION

4

What is your moral code, in relation to right and wrong?

Richard Dawkins

I follow the same moral code as most thinking people. It's put together by complicated cultural influences from the history of human culture. Religions, democratic decisions, moral philosophy, literature, a whole lot of influences from the past, probably including some primitive Darwinian influences as well, feed into this melting pot, and give us a kind of conscience based on moral values, such as it's wrong to hurt other individuals, it's wrong to kill other individuals, it's wrong to cause suffering. These are complicated issues because some values contradict others. But people who live now in the beginning of the 21st century, educated people, tend to have a pretty common set of moral values. They tend to think that slavery is wrong, that racial discrimination is wrong, that one should do all in one's power to minimize suffering and maximize happiness. That has not always been true, but it tends to be true of educated people today, whether or not they are religious.

"One should do all in one's power to minimize suffering and maximize happiness."

RICHARD DAWKINS

Gianfranco Ferre

What is right and what is wrong in my mind may offend the freedom of someone else. I don't judge the way anyone thinks and I believe that one should not take away the freedom of another human being. A moral code is something inside oneself.

Anjelica Huston

I think the moral code is about not trying to hurt other people, which in the end comes down to trying not to hurt oneself. For me, it's an ongoing situation how your morality comes into play and what it's based on. It's very subjective. There are things one reacts to prudishly, whereas you may take a *laissez-faire* attitude to other things that might be twice as shocking to somebody else. "Do unto others as you would have them do unto you," is a pretty good code for behavior in general.

Charles Le Gai Eaton

My moral code is Islamic Law, the Shariah, inescapable whether I obey it meticulously or not. I do not believe in the possibility of a secular morality based on "feelings," likes, and dislikes. It is as changeable as fashion in women's clothing. Even if it is basically sound, at least in some respects it has no stability. Most human beings are capable of almost anything under certain circumstances. The reason that you and I have never committed murder is that we have never experienced circumstances which made it appear the only solution, which is why I am unwilling to condemn people in terms of their actions. It is not so much what we do that matters, as what we are. Though what we do usually reflects what we are.

"It is not so much what we do that matters, as what we are. Though what we do usually reflects what we are."

CHARLES LE GAI EATON

David Frost

Right and wrong is a function, I suppose, of conscience, and is a function of what you know and what you feel. I think that people tend to know and have an innate sense of good and evil, and it's up to them what they want to do with it. When they are doing something that is wrong, they sometimes persist with it although it can make them very unhappy. But I think even people who try to ignore this sense of right and wrong feel affected by it. Not hurting other people's feelings, I would have thought a basic tenet. Making a contribution to people's lives, that's another priority. Not wasting time, and using the opportunities you have been given to the full.

Jools Holland

It's important to be fair and straight. And it's important to do things that improve the quality of life for everybody. Artists' responsibility is first of all to their art, and if they are true artists, their art will improve things for people around them anyway—by opening their eyes or ears, or just making them have a dance, or momentarily taking them away from the world.

Paulo Coelho

There are two ways to express the moral code: the Christian and the Jewish way. I am closer to the Jewish one, although I am a Christian. The Christians say: "Love your neighbor as you love yourself." This is a sentence that can create a lot of misunderstanding. You may not love yourself, or you may love yourself so much that you try to impose your values on your neighbors. Love is also a matter of sharing. So the margin to err in this concept is gigantic, because half of the crimes that humankind has committed were based on righteousness, the idea that we should impose our values on our neighbors. The Jewish concept is much clearer. It is: "Don't do to your neighbor, what you don't want him to do to yourself." Then you have a very precise and clear picture of what is right and what is wrong, because you put yourself in the role of your neighbor. The negative sentence clarifies the situation much more than the positive sentence. The moment that you step beyond this line, that you start to impose your values, or your ideas, or whatever, even if you have good intentions, it is wrong. So let people live their lives.

Sharon Stone

I don't really believe in morals. I think morals are something created by society to control people into sheeplike behavior. I think that ethics come from the truth and dignity in your heart.

Seyyed Hossein Nasr

I believe that the criteria for determining right and wrong in this world are originally given to us by God, not only through external revelation, which is absolutely essential, but also through the inner revelation, which is the intelligence associated in all traditions with the heart. I believe that upon the very substance of our soul as God has created us, there has been written what good is, but that primordial substance has become covered by forgetfulness, by the fall of man, by what Christianity calls original sin and other religions call by other names. Intelligence does not function in a wholesome way within fallen man.

Many people in the modern world say that they have no interest in religion but know what good and evil are. They assert that they are very good and moral human beings and that you can have agnostic or atheistic morality. The reality of the matter is that what they call morality, based on distinction between good and evil, is the inheritance of several thousand years of religion, first Christianity and before that the Greco-Roman religions and other religions. For example, if there is no ultimate reality, why is human life sacred? Why not disrespect human life? Why should one not kill a neighbor who is useless?

Take this debate that is going on right now on the sanctity of human life, which I accept completely. If human life, like all life, is nothing more than the result of electrons banging against each other, or molecules in a soup, which have then evolved à la Darwin, a view that I do not accept at all, then why is human life sacred? If life just came out of the soup of original super-molecules after the Big Bang, what is sacred about it? There still lingers the idea that human life is inviolable; it is sanctified and so on. But such a view would be based on sheer sentimentality if one rejects the sacred origin of life. The reason mankind has survived is because of the heritage and the teachings of Christianity in the West or Islam and other religions in the East, based on a theology and metaphysics which emphasize the divine origin of all existence and especially the sacred character of human life. The question of good and evil is a very fundamental and basic one, but it can never be answered except by having recourse to something that transcends the level of the material world, a science that is none other than metaphysics, the science of divine reality. This is an important crisis for Western civilization, because a part of humanity, especially in Europe more than in America, has become highly secularized. In such a situation the question remains what the source of morality is. Do we vote for morality, just vote for what is good and evil as we vote every few years for other issues in a climate which is based on ever-changing circumstances? Do you ask a number of wise men to formulate acceptable ethics? They will not even agree among themselves as to the nature of these ethics. And even if they did, who is going to listen to them? This is a critical issue.

Farah Pahlavi

The essential values and moral codes, which have been handed down throughout the ages, have changed with time. I believe in the Charter of Human Rights, and living with the values therein brings me inner peace.

Shimon Peres

If you can be kind and understanding to other people, you are basically on the right track. One cannot be perfect, because all of us have our own problems and none of us has full control of ourselves, so right and wrong depends on choosing a positive attitude. A great problem in life is couples. We are made to live each of us individually, yet we cannot exist just by remaining individual. So we have to enter into a relationship, which is extremely difficult, but then be careful not to hurt the other party. Many people in my life have helped me and many have disappointed me. But I would rather make mistakes by trusting people than make mistakes by mistrusting them.

"One cannot be perfect. . ."

SHIMON PERES

Sophia Loren

Right and wrong are not fixed principles. If we looked at morality on a broad scale, we could say that right is whatever benefits humanity and makes people happy, wrong is what tends to affect humankind in a harmful way.

Una M. Kroll

My moral code is based upon the Ten Commandments of the Old Testament in Exodus: 20:1–17 and upon the Sermon on the Mount (Matthew 5–7). The Ten Commandments provide me with simple rules of behavior. The Sermon on the Mount provides me with a commentary on these commandments, which expands them into ideals. I know that I cannot actually attain those ideals, but by keeping them foremost in my mind I am helped to behave in ways that lead me to become a more whole human being than I would otherwise be.

Emma Sergeant

This is a tricky question for me because I have done things that are strictly speaking wrong. (They felt quite right at the time.) So I'm not one to start talking about high values and morals here. I've always ended up hurting people. I've tried not to, but I have. I've probably been cruel. I think one just has to do the best that one can in the circumstances, and be responsible about picking up the pieces and trying to put things right if you feel you've done wrong.

Ed Begley Jr.

I think it's important to have some ethics in your life and behave in an honorable fashion. It's just a miserable way to live otherwise. You're constantly scrambling and trying to make up for lies and half-truths and innuendo. It's just so much easier to remember the truth, and to live a life that is caring and generous toward others. Not just other people, other creatures. It's a good idea to tread as lightly as you can. Why must you leave a trail of carnage behind you, to just go about the business of living? I don't think it's necessary.

Mangosuthu Buthelezi

Zulus have a moral code which is not very different from the Ten Commandments.

Nelson Mandela

These things are sometimes not absolute. They are relative. People who don't respect other religions are responsible for a great deal of instability in the world. To use religion for the purpose of challenging other religions is grossly wrong. The important thing is to respect religious convictions; whether you believe in them or not, respect them. Because if you don't, you will never make peace with people who belong to that religious order.

"To use religion for the purpose of challenging other religions is grossly wrong."

NELSON MANDELA

David Lynch

It says in the Bible, "Judge not lest ye be judged." Desire is so strong for certain things that you don't find out that what you've done is wrong until afterward, when it is kind of too late. Sometimes you know up front but you can fool yourself. It's so tricky, that I guess you have to remember sometimes when you got burned before so you don't do it again. All you can do is to really and truly expand your awareness and consciousness. Everything is right as long as you don't hurt anybody. Of course, you can never really please everybody and it is hard enough to please yourself. I'm not talking about not only hurting your family, but I'm talking about your surrounding people. People for me are important things, living things; people, animals—as long as they don't get hurt everything is okay.

Dadi Janki with Sister Jayanti

Morality is not a question of belief. Each person's conscience will tell them what is right and wrong, what is false or true, sin or charity. Human beings are in bondage to three things:

1. Sometimes our own conscience tells us there is something wrong, but we suppress this and follow the views of the world.
2. We have many desires of our own which lead to things such as jealousy and conflict, but we still give way to them.
3. We are obligated and bound to our relations and friends.

When there is a relationship with God, an inner power awakens our conscience and we follow that. This is true and we must do it. Throughout my life I have considered lies, theft, cheating, and gossip to be sins. If you say to people these are wrong, they will try to agree but will continue to do them.

Gore Vidal

Who is to decide right or wrong? It is a very human concept and a very unclear one. That's like pretending you are still in school. You've passed the exam, you've flunked the exam.

Bob Geldof

You have to test this random individual consciousness called Bob or whoever to its absolute limits without hurting anyone else or trying your best not to. I am capable of doing more than some people and less than others. You experiment to see what you can do, and then at the end hopefully you've exhausted the potential of self. What I would ideally like is that my last conscious thought would be, "That was interesting."

Robert Fisk

I think you know what is the right thing to do in certain circumstances, so does one need a code? If I see people who are wounded, I try to help them. If I see people who are trying to escape from danger, I try to get them out. If I see something terrible that has happened, I write about it and I try to say who the bad guys are and who the innocent are. I don't have a code for that.

> "It's obvious that ultimately there is no right and wrong in reality."
>
> HARRY DEAN STANTON

Harry Dean Stanton

Well, it's obvious that ultimately there is no right and wrong in reality. We see the horror and bliss and the good and the beautiful. The good and the horror have always been there. You don't embrace the evil or the horror but you have to accept it as a manifestation of the totality of existence. My moral code is very, very simple: don't lie to anybody, including yourself, and don't steal. It's not a question of right and wrong, it is a matter of intelligence. You don't lie, because it's stupid; and you don't steal, because it's a stupid thing to do.

His Holiness The Dalai Lama

Strong moral ethics are as concomitantly crucial to a man of politics as they are to a man of religion, for dangerous consequences are foreseen when our politicians and those who rule forget their moral principles and convictions. Irrespective of whether we are a believer or an agnostic, whether we believe in God or karma, moral ethics is a code that everyone is able to pursue.

"Sometimes you have to quiet your life to hear what is the right thing to do."

BONO

Bono

You know instinctively, always, what's the right thing to do. And the greatest enemy of that instinct is the din of too many choices. Noise. I think of that story in the Bible of Elijah who was told he should go up a hill and wait to hear from God. A mighty wind springs up and he thinks: "Here it comes, God's on his way." Then there's an earthquake, but no word from God. Then comes a great fire and he thinks God will speak from the fire, but no. The wind calms down and in the stillness he hears God's voice. My idea of that is sometimes you have to quiet your life to hear what is the right thing to do.

Michael Radford

I believe in one thing, the ultimate goodness of man. For some reason we have within us an altruistic desire to do good, and whoever does not is profoundly unhappy. That is my moral code. Many people have said to me that to be successful you have to cheat and steal. That may be true to be successful in a materialistic world, but I don't live in a materialistic world. Look at me, I am a film director who is supposed to be earning millions of dollars and I don't because I don't care. The moral paradoxes of our lives—what is good in the short term and what is good in the long term? What is goodness—to me those questions are much more interesting than thinking about an afterlife.

Robert Graham

There is a structure of collective morals which is pretty definite whether it's based on Eastern or Western religion. For instance, you do not go out killing people, stealing, and doing all that stuff, so that's pretty clear-cut. But then you sometimes have to steal, sometimes you have to kill, sometimes you have to do all those things. So I would say you do anything that feels right, which comes down to your own sense of shame or conscience, and it's not just your conscience but also the environment you live in. You can have a personal conscience, an artistic conscience which I would term to be religious and spiritual in an artist. But then you have to have a collective conscience too—you have to be part of this whole thing. So sometimes when it feels good for you to do something, it's still not right and you have to take that into account. You are subject to consequences.

Michael Fitzpatrick

I have an obligation to follow my dream, first and foremost, with the express purpose and realization that in doing so I am serving humanity to the fullest of my capacities. I have been given a gift, a gift that must be given, over and over. I've committed my life to using music to bring "peace" to people. Peace is a feeling, like compassion, that becomes a moral compass.

Alfredo Guevara

I believe that the worst enemy of humanity is ignorance, which is the main motor of indifference, of people living banal, empty lives. I believe that by cultivating people spiritually, raising their ethical and cultural education, refining their sensibilities, we come closer to humanizing them. If we can avoid the dulling process of routine that is one of the main sources of ignorance, and which can affect even the most cultured of men and women, evil will not have many doors open to it. I think that the human quality, the refinement of the spirit, lead to the capacity for love and not only the love of another person. I believe, like the Greeks, like Plato, that love, beauty, and truth make mankind good. These are the antidotes to evil, and they are interconnected truths.

"I believe, like the Greeks, like Plato, that love, beauty and truth make mankind good."

ALFREDO GUEVARA

Zac Goldsmith

Unfashionable though it is, I do believe that there are very clear "rights" and very clear "wrongs." An act that contributes to the destruction of this Earth is wrong in the sense that it undermines the livelihoods of others, both human and otherwise. Very simply, it is not good enough merely to behave nicely toward one another unless that kindness is based on an understanding of the bigger picture.

Frei Betto

Everything that defends, protects, and serves life—God's major gift—is positive. Everything that offends against, oppresses, and excludes life is negative. Love is right. The absence of love is wrong.

Albina du Boisrouvray

What is wrong is disrespect and disregard for the dignity of anyone or anything living—that is to say, human beings, animals, the planet. It is respect for life that is the very first thing in my moral code. For me that goes a long way: rescuing orphans, breaking my neck to go to very horrible places, risking sometimes my life for something that has to do with respect for someone else's life or dignity. I feel love is a factor of morality. It's a sin not to give love to life. It's not our burden to take on everything, but I think we have to feel that we have a responsibility within our small lives, our small sphere, and an obligation to try to carry it out, especially toward those who are not so privileged. Also, to me, courage is the criterion of what is good and what is bad, courage and integrity. Whenever there's a path you have to choose, you ask yourself, "Am I going to be courageous or a coward; am I going to act with integrity or dubious motives?" If you choose integrity and courage you are never wrong, it will pay off in the long run whereas the other attitude won't. It's a yardstick by which to go.

Jack Nicholson

All the platitudes of life seem to apply to morality: "Do unto others," the golden rule. Like any other higher principle, you subscribe to it but you don't always follow it. Some of the simplest principles—for instance, that it's better to give than to receive—people accept as a conventional wisdom. But if you actually are doing that, it will prove itself true or not. We live in a worldly society that has its own life and by which we are all influenced. We all swim in the same river, and that's ever-changing.

Jilly Cooper

I think right and wrong is incredibly important. I think the most important thing in the world is to be kind and not hurt people, and to protect the weak and the innocent: animals, children, and grown-ups when they need it; all creatures great and small, in fact.

Steve Vai

I have had the fortunate experience of meeting and talking with a holy man when I was in India. I asked him: "How do we do the right thing when we know we are doing the wrong thing?" He said: "It's very simple. Before you do anything ask yourself if it's spiritually healthy or not." I think that's quite a lofty moral code and something to strive to live by.

QUESTION

5

Do you believe you have a destiny, and do you see yourself as here to fulfill it?

Zac Goldsmith

Everyone has a biological and social destiny. Our role is, I believe, to live in a manner that is supportive of the larger community. Just as the heart must cooperate with the lungs, so the individual should cooperate with the family, the family with the community, and the community with society and the natural world. From my own point of view, I am driven to fight for a restoration of sanity in the manner in which my species relates to its environment. That is my role and, for whatever reason, I believe that is the only option available to me if I am to live a satisfied life. Whether individuals are born with an express destiny, or whether they themselves with the help of their friends, family, and environment sculpt that destiny, I do not know. In likelihood, while I believe genes are responsible for many of a person's characteristics, the context in which that person has matured is equally, if not more, important. I imagine only the hand that one is dealt is preordained. It is up to the individual to decide how to play it.

Gore Vidal

There's no destiny, other than what you invent. I'm one of the original existentialists in the United States. I was doing it unconsciously long before I read Sartre. I knew that nothing mattered, other than the fact that we attached value to it. I became a writer because I wanted to, because of my DNA. I believe in genetic inheritance to a point. That's what I was intended to be. I would much rather have been the president, something that every Gore, including John Huston, has wanted to be. But some of us have to settle for writing books or being film directors.

"Our free will is intertwined with our destiny. In a sense, through our free will we fulfill our destinies."

SEYYED HOSSEIN NASR

Seyyed Hossein Nasr

I believe in destiny in the metaphysical sense, but I do not believe that it annuls our free will. Those who you might say were "naturalists" in ancient Greek thought denied free will. Christianity opposed Greek understanding of destiny very strongly by speaking about the person of God who loves us and saves us and can interfere in history. Islam, even more than Christianity, emphasizes what is called *qada* and *qadar*—that is, God's foreknowledge of all that will happen and His power to implement what He has ordained for us in this world.

Other groups have denied free will on the basis of a particular argument such as dialectical materialism, psychological behavioralism, biological and chemical determination, or philosophical determinism. In various religions, one finds the voices of both determinism and free will. But without freedom of the will there is no moral responsibility. Our free will is conditioned by many things. Sometimes we knock our head against a door but the door never opens. At other times, just a tap and the door opens. Some things that you want to accomplish are never accomplished; other things are accomplished easily. That is related to our destiny. But there is for human beings the immediate consciousness of freedom at particular moments of life when we decide something. So our free will is intertwined with our destiny. In a sense, through our free will we fulfill our destinies.

A happy person is a person whose free actions correspond to his destiny. I once said somewhere, although I am not a Buddhist or a Hindu, happy is the person whose karma is his dharma. Dharma is a wonderfully rich word in Sanskrit, and means duty, vocation, path, and also destiny, while karma is related to our actions and reactions caused by those actions. From the religious point of view, destiny is God's will for us. In a practical manner, to fulfill one's destiny is to surrender oneself to the will of God, and the surrender must come through our free will. So we are free to the extent that we submit our freedom to God's will.

Shimon Peres

I think I have an opportunity but not a destiny. I think I have to catch that opportunity and handle it properly.

Nelson Mandela

I don't believe it is my destiny but my duty to help people where I can offer help. I believe that as a human being there are certain things that you must do in order to improve the living conditions of humanity. The greatest challenge facing us is that of poverty. If you can contribute toward driving the factors of poverty backward, then you have served society. Because there is nothing more humiliating than poverty: it is an assault on human dignity. Our duty, therefore, is to make sure that people crawl out of poverty, so they can look after their children, and their families, and the community. I have no doubt that one day the world will reach that position. You didn't have the values in the past world that you have today, where so many people condemn poverty and want everybody to be on the same level, both educationally and otherwise.

"I don't believe it is my destiny but my duty to help people where I can offer help."

NELSON MANDELA

Alfredo Guevara

I believe human beings create their own destiny and, for me, the proof of this is that the unwittingly ignorant have no power over their own lives whereas the cultured, refined, sensitive person constructs their own role in life.

Bob Geldof

I don't really accept the idea of destiny. It implies that if someone is having a lousy time, they're destined to have it, but that's not true. A set of circumstances makes someone end up outside a supermarket with a sleeping bag around them, homeless. They're circumstances: destiny didn't mean it to happen. Equally true, if something fantastic happens to you, it is probably not destiny, it is you pinning that idea on nondescript events in your life.

Una M. Kroll

I believe that I am here to fulfill God's purposes through living my human life and to be happy with him in heaven. My idea of heaven is that it is union with God and that it begins here on Earth. As someone who feels called to live my life as one of continuous prayer, I feel "called" by God to live it in a certain way, as a priest in the Church of Wales and as a woman who has given her life over to God, first as a married woman for 30 years and now as a solitary in life-vows.

David Frost

I don't believe that we have a preordained destiny. The word "destiny" is a bit grand. I believe you have a set of opportunities, forks in the road, crossroads, and if you take those opportunities, you fulfill not necessarily your destiny, you fulfill your potential, your aspirations. If you take the wrong turnings and reject opportunities, then obviously you don't fulfill those aspirations. I am reminded of that story of a man who is shipwrecked on a desert island who prays to God to rescue him. Soon after a native boat comes by, and indicates would he like to be picked up. He says, "No, God is going to save me." Then a larger boat comes by, and then a liner, and he repeats, "No, God is going to save me." God doesn't save him and he dies and goes to heaven, and says to God, "I prayed to you, God, to save me and you let me down." And God says, "What do you mean, first of all I sent you a native boat, then a larger ship, I even sent you a liner." I guess God helps those who help themselves.

Charles Le Gai Eaton

I believe in ultimate predestination, although free will is also real at a certain level. We have to accept a contradiction that does not make sense to us—but why should we expect everything to make sense to us? What we do, the things that happen to us, the people we meet, all are a fulfillment of our destiny. That is why we are here: to play out the role assigned to us before this theater was created.

Jools Holland

I think the answer is yes, people do have a destiny, but none of us knows what destiny is. I think the more you relax and allow yourself just to be part of it, and just go with the flow, the easier it is. I have had my own patron saint looking after me. I never particularly wanted to travel, for example, but I've done that because it's just come to me.

Dadi Janki with Sister Jayanti

I give thanks to God that He has made me belong to Him and given me a special role in serving the world. I constantly feel the blessings of all, and there is nothing else in my heart except gratitude. I have a guarantee that I will always be a companion of God and be able to benefit the world, and this is what my purpose in this life is.

Paulo Coelho

I believe everyone has a destiny. I wrote a book based on this concept, *The Alchemist,* in which the main character called his destiny the personal legend. For many years I tried to find an answer as to what I am doing here, what is my destiny. I got thousands of answers from different religions and philosophical schools, but I don't think any one of them is true. I think we should respect the mystery of being here, be humble, and say that we don't fully understand what is happening. But I know I am close to my destiny when I am enthusiastic about life. Life is almost a living being, a gigantic body around your own life, as if you are a cell of this soul.

When you have enthusiasm you are close to what I call your personal agent, you are doing something that is meaningful to you. When you are close to your destiny you are affecting the soul of the world. Destiny is like a train on which you are going toward death. In this train you can move from first class to second class, from a comfortable place to a very uncomfortable one, you have several possibilities in the wagons of the train, but you are on the same rails. It is a matter of moving inside the train. This is destiny, it is not fate.

"I know I am close to my destiny when I am enthusiastic about life."

PAULO COELHO

Robert Fisk

No, I never think about a personal destiny at all. But we all live under the malign influence of history. I certainly do. In the period of two years after the First World War, my father's generation created the borders of the Balkans, Northern Ireland, and the Middle East, and I spent my entire professional life watching some of the people there burn in all those three places. So I don't know what comes in the future, but the past can sure destroy us.

Bono

I believe you create your own destiny. You choose it every day. For me, one of the most important ideas is that you can begin again. It's one of the reasons I am attracted to the idea of the poorest countries having their debts to the richest canceled. The ability to start again is enshrined in any worthy philosophy. Putting the past behind you doesn't always means ignoring the past, but learning from it and moving on.

> "I believe you create your own destiny. You choose it every day."
>
> BONO

Anjelica Huston

I think it was my destiny to be born who I am, and to live with the cards I have been dealt. Sometimes I question, of course, the meaning of life, what my mission is, what my mission can be. I know my mission hasn't been to bear children, so I think my mission in some way has been, and hopefully is or will be, an effort to make people see both sides of the situation.

Jack Nicholson

Well, I am a World War II child, so I had a strong generational sense of heroism, a desire for greatness. These were normal ambitions. My background has me wanting to do some good, but by the time you're where I am, you're not sure if you ever will, ever did, or knew what it was to begin with.

Michael Radford

I've always believed that I have a destiny. Time's running out, actually, and clearly I may have been wasting my time. But right from when I was a little boy I felt I had a destiny, which was put into perspective when I got to Hollywood. Someone crudely asked me, "Are you into the money thing or the fame thing?" So I said, "Well I have a sense of destiny." And they said, "Oh, the fame thing!"

Harry Dean Stanton

It's all predestined. Nobody's in charge, it's all just one huge miraculous manifestation. Comes out of nothing and goes back into nothing. We are predisposed to do what we do. I had nothing to do with what has happened to my life. Everything that has happened to my life, or yours, or any human being's had to happen that way and nobody was in charge of it. We want to hang on and be attached to this concept that we are a person, that we are an identity, and we are separate and will live personally forever. It's another projection of ego, a myth, an illusion, like Santa Claus.

Steve Vai

Yes, I believe we all have destinies and that you can't fool fate. There are those who believe that time, in its sequential linear form, is really an illusion and that all things coexist in the here and now. Oddly enough, this concept seems to make crystal-clear sense to me. I believe that every living creature's life is important because it's a particular stepping-stone in their spiritual evolution. Not one person or living creature is more important than another. That is why we are created equal. We are all aspiring to the same goal and we will all get there eventually.

> "We all have a destiny, and what we get to decide is with how much integrity we meet that destiny."
>
> SHARON STONE

Emma Sergeant

I feel that fulfilling my destiny is almost too arrogant a way of putting it. I feel that my duty is just to fulfill my day and God will show me the way. Great things are thrust upon us sometimes. I feel we have a series of choices and there's a chemical makeup in all of us. Sometimes you feel you're carrying radioactive matter instead of blood in your veins and you're about to explode because there's so much that you want to achieve and want to do. How frustrated you feel that it never quite happens, it's never quite the right time. You can't understand why because of twists of fate you are always missing out on what you perceive to be your destiny. Timing is everything. Sometimes you have to be patient so you feel a sense of destiny. One has got to accept when things go wrong, that in fact they're really going right. Then you will understand that there is a rhythm to the world, and if you can follow that rhythm, all things will come to you.

Peter Ustinov

No, I never really thought I was a man of destiny at all. The nice things that happened to me in my life took me by surprise, which is a kind of proof to my mind that I never expected anything and I never aimed for anything. I never expected to be knighted; I never expected to be a member of the French Academy of all things; or the Académie des Beaux Arts. I never expected half the wonderful things to happen that did happen to me.

Farah Pahlavi

I feel one is destined, but I do not know what percentage of destiny comes into your life. I remember once I said to my eldest daughter, Farinaz, when I was very busy with things to do with my country, and tired: "I do not know what I am doing, is it my choice or is it my destiny?" She told me mine was a destiny that did not leave me much choice. Of course, today I could have a choice and accept all the consequences. I could say I do not want to do anything about my country and compatriots and just live my life with my family, but there would be reactions and then my choice to accept the reactions. In any case, I care about my country. As my daughter said, it is not an easy choice.

David Lynch

Yes, I think I have a destiny. Destiny is sometimes tied to desires, your desires to fulfill certain things, but I also think that everybody's destiny is to try to attain that full-blown, unbounded awareness, consciousness. The road is really all about that, so you can live life with a full deck of cards.

Sophia Loren

Honestly, I don't believe that I have a destiny that I am here to fulfill. Destiny is generated mostly by our actions. We are responsible for what we do.

Mangosuthu Buthelezi

I believe this completely, that I was born with a destiny. When God created me there was a purpose, and a mission that I must fulfill while I am on this Earth.

Michael Fitzpatrick

I believe I have a destiny. I definitely have the sense of being a bridge, for musical generations, across musical generations. A sense that there's a new music here for me to find. A sense of music's potential to heal the world. Having two instruments to work with, an acoustic cello built 100 years ago and a five-string electric cello built in Seattle, gives structure to this sense of destiny. I think growing up in nature helped keep me connected to my destiny. And having great parents, artistic parents; great sisters, a photographer and a violist; my grandmother, Rose, a concert pianist who could play any tune in any key, by ear, better than anyone I've ever heard.

When I was 17, I had what I can only describe as a mystical experience. On stage in front of 2,000 people in a concert hall in North Carolina, I had an 80-piece orchestra behind me and was in the middle of the solo of the cello concerto that I was playing, by Édouard Lalo. All of a sudden, what felt like the roof of the auditorium opened up and this funnel cloud of energy, what seemed like a cosmic beam, started descending from above, coming straight toward me. Then I felt my whole body/mind suffuse in a glorious golden light. I heard a new sound, a golden sound come from the cello. For the remainder of the performance I found myself in some timeless space, each note filled with this energy. Afterward, I knew something had happened that was extraordinary, something that forever changed my life and did give me this sense that I had been touched by God and given a specific gift through music.

Frei Betto

I believe you devise your own destiny based on your living environment and embraced values, and on opportunities in life.

His Holiness The Dalai Lama

As a Buddhist monk, the cultivation of compassion is an important part of my daily practice. One aspect involves merely sitting quietly in my room, meditating. That can be very good and very comfortable, but the true aim of cultivating compassion is to develop the courage to think of others and to do something for them. For example, as the Dalai Lama I have a responsibility to my people, some of whom are living as refugees and some of whom have remained in Tibet under Chinese occupation. This responsibility means that I have to confront and deal with many problems.

"As the Dalai Lama I have a responsibility to my people."

HIS HOLINESS THE DALAI LAMA

Robert Graham

I think I have a destiny. It's a kind of package you have been dealt. You look at it and say I can squander it or I can develop it. Not everyone gets the same package, so you are responsible for that certain program that somebody else didn't get, and you've got to put it to use. If you don't, then you are not fulfilling that particular accident of fate. Some kind of DNA combination.

"You've got to put it to use. If you don't, then you are not fulfilling that particular accident of fate."

ROBERT GRAHAM

Albina du Boisrouvray

I feel we all have a destiny, but not a set one. The path to fulfilling your destiny is very difficult to find when you are young, and it takes a lot of experience of life to be able to do that. It's like weaving a pattern when you can freely choose the colors of your threads. At the end of the day your pattern is going to be your destiny, but the way you weave with the green thread or the red thread is going to have consequences, ripple-effects that you cannot foresee.

Gianfranco Ferre

I think destiny is like a white horse that is crossing in front of you, and you have to decide to make your destiny by jumping on it. You have to create your own personality in order to make this jump and change your life. I believe one is in control of one's destiny. I've achieved what I wanted to do, even at the cost of taking risks, although at the same time you have to be conscious of your own capacity.

Richard Dawkins

I believe that individuals have personal ambitions. A word like destiny makes it sound rather grand, and it can also make it sound as though the destiny is somehow imposed from outside, as though there is some influence that forces one to a particular way of life. I don't find that a helpful way of looking at it. I prefer to say that I feel like a free agent who has ambitions and desires, aims and goals.

Ilana Goor

Yes, I think I have a destiny with my art. That is the only thing I know how to do.

Ed Begley Jr.

I don't know much about destiny, I just do what's before me. It's kind of a Buddhist notion, I suppose, to do that instead of having all these grand schemes, like saving the world. I'm very fortunate, I have a little baby girl and that's my joy, to be able to raise another child. I have two grown children and to be able to do that again is a great gift. So I guess that's my destiny, to try to raise some nice people.

QUESTION

6

What has life taught you so far?

Frei Betto

Life has taught me that there is no salvation other than love. I was jailed twice under the Brazilian military dictatorship, four years the second time. I never hated my torturers or jailers. There's no merit in this. I just realized that hatred first destroys those who hate, not those who are hated. Life is a very beautiful adventure, full of love. It is a pity that so many people around us are excluded from it. Until there is justice, freedom, and peace for the whole of mankind, I will not be fully happy.

"Life has taught me that there is no salvation other than love."

FREI BETTO

Charles Le Gai Eaton

Life has taught me to accept my own foolishness and the inescapable contradictions in my own character. To accept that it was not my destiny to be the sort of person I would have liked to be. To try to see people as they see themselves—the only way to understand them. To appreciate the distinctions between one shade of gray and another. To believe that if you like people, it is probable that they will like you. To trust people, partly because it is too much bother to go around full of distrust, and to accept that being let down is among the normal vicissitudes of life and you only harm yourself by bitterness. To accept my inherent laziness, since I have never managed to overcome it—so why worry? Enduring amazement at the human capacity for self-deception and self-justification, a tendency so universal that I wonder if it is not necessary to human survival in this world. Finally, when possible, to rejoice rather than moan!

Michael Radford

Life's taught me so far one very important lesson, which is that it is not a rehearsal. I think that is the best way to put it. You can watch life going by, particularly when you are young, when it seems to be endless, and realize that it has passed you by before you know it. Coupled with that is the sense that when you make a fundamental choice in your life it is usually not at a moment when you are aware that you are making such a choice. You usually do it in passing and you realize years later that, at that moment, there was a huge turning point in your life. It is very strange how that works, that the key decisions which have made you happy or sad are just ones that somehow never seem to be important at the time. But life has also taught me that you have to live every single day as though it were your last.

Actually, at this age, I have discovered that one of the things when one is young is that life is full of infinite possibilities, you can imagine yourself as different things. You continue to do that until one day you wake up and you say, "Oh my God, I am a film director, this is my life, this is the one I have chosen." I am not going to be an around-the-world-racing yachtsman, I am not going to be a sheep farmer, the things that you fantasize about occasionally. I am not going to spend my life in Bombay, all the things that "could have been," even 10 years ago. Suddenly you realize "this is it." This is the one life I had, and how short it was really.

Bono

I've learned that I'm a slow learner, but when eventually the penny drops I hold on to it very tightly. I catch it in my hand and I hold on to it. I just wish I was quicker on the uptake.

Ilana Goor

Life's taught me to be gentler, because not everyone is the same. I've learned to have more patience, to try to understand more, because we are not all alike. Also to look more carefully, to control my feelings. And I always say: one thing about aging, the older you become, the more about life you know. If you knew all those things when you were young, your life would have been much more pleasant. But life is a process of growing, so it has taught me to give respect to a person, not to a position. Because the minute I feel you are sincere and you care and you really believe in what you are doing, you're fine with me.

"One thing about aging, the older you become, the more about life you know."

ILANA GOOR

PAULO COELHO

I've learned to see myself as being on a pilgrimage: to travel light, contact other pilgrims, be simple, look around, realize that God is in everything, have a target in mind. There is a circulating energy between being a master and being a disciple. If you only try to be a master, you are lost; if you only try to be a disciple, you are lost. My target is to keep a constant communion with God, understanding that joy and pain are the two faces of the same coin, and so not trying to understand God but to be in contact, to have a glimpse at least once or twice a day.

ALBINA DU BOISROUVRAY

With the loss of my son, who was not only my big, big love but also my way of giving out love, I've learned that to go on being a loving person you have to rely on your inner self. You cannot base your capacity for love entirely on a single loving relationship, because if one element of that relationship disappears you are completely destabilized and at a loss. So I think a wise rule of life is to try to become your own solid self, from which you can then give out love and really give it. Then you don't need to depend on an exchange of love. The other thing I've learned is the precariousness of everything and the shortness of time. Time is very, very short to do things: to enjoy people, to enjoy the ones you love, to find your path, your colors. You never, never know if what is here today will be here tomorrow or what state it will be in tomorrow, and that goes for all your life. There's the saying, "Look at the glass as half-full, not as half-empty." It's a good image, and important.

Nelson Mandela

What I have learned from life is to be grateful that I am alive and can serve society.

Gianfranco Ferre

Life is what has been given to you, you have to be free in your life, you have to believe in something and you have to try not to compromise, otherwise you will not be happy.

Dadi Janki with Sister Jayanti

I am still learning many things. Among them that I must not compare myself with anyone else, and that I must have no trace of ego or attachment to anything that is mine. I have also learned from God to have humility and seek to benefit all. Everyone is hungry for love.

Farah Pahlavi

I have learned not to feel sorry for myself. Life is a struggle for everybody. I follow the old saying, "God grant me the serenity to accept the things I cannot change, the courage to change the things I can, and the wisdom to know the difference." I also attach importance to the French saying, "Les conseilleurs ne sont pas les payeurs," which means: "Those who give advice don't pay the price." I have learned that you can lose everything in life but what you should not lose is your dignity as a human being, otherwise you have lost the battle of life.

"I have learned that you can lose everything in life but what you should not lose is your dignity as a human being, otherwise you have lost the battle of life."

FARAH PAHLAVI

Emma Sergeant

One lesson is to be humble and you will be rewarded. If you are talented, you've got to work twice as hard on your soul as on your craft, because it would be so easy to do what's easy. You've got to push yourself harder and understand that God put that spot on your forehead. You are just a red ant; you'd be nothing if it weren't for God.

Alfredo Guevara

Life has taught me that it is very hard, sometimes tragic, but that it is worth living. There is nothing more wonderful than creating, and I am talking not only about art or science but of man's potential, to be creative even in the simplest moments in life. Looking after others, being loved, activating the conscience of pupils . . . it's a wonderful moment in life, when one feels that a very young person is waking up to curiosity about areas of knowledge and sensitivity. This transmission can give rise to a feeling that life is not only wonderful but that it is more than justified.

"There is nothing more wonderful than creating. . .to be creative even in the simplest moments in life."

ALFREDO GUEVARA

Robert Fisk

What do you mean by life? The experience of being a journalist? I think the experience of living through the civil war in Lebanon taught me to be very hard, to take decisions that I would normally find very difficult to take, and to take them immediately. In a war you have to take decisions with your life: whether to run across the road, whether to go to a particular town or not, or whether to stay indoors or travel when it's dangerous. You don't go through ages of indecision, because you taught yourself that certain decisions have to be made and if you're wrong, your life will end.

Life has taught me to value history. My father taught me to be interested in history and to like books. I think the printed page is very important. I don't use the Internet, I don't know how to, and I don't use e-mail. So if you are looking for something that's important to me, it would be books and history. I've learned a lot from history.

Sophia Loren

Life has taught me to be happy for the good things I have achieved, and also the precious value of family.

David Frost

A great quote of my father's was, "Even a stopped clock is right twice a day." Everyone has something to teach you if you are prepared to hunt for it, and learn from it, even a stopped clock. That's important in the sense of treating everyone you meet in a similar way. I've also learned that when things come along that seem almost too good to be true, they usually are too good to be true. In a phrase: "Always look a gift horse in the mouth."

Jools Holland

The most important thing life's taught me is that although I learn new things all the time, I don't really know a lot. If you think you know what's going on, then you've made a very big mistake. I've also found that things often don't work out if you try too hard. People can only do what they can do; they shouldn't feel bad about what they can't do. You can learn things from anything that's going on around you and from the most unexpected people. Not everybody has something illuminating or brilliant to say, but most people have some point to make and you dismiss it at your peril. Another thing I've learned is that it's important to know when to say the right thing and when not to say anything, and that the simplest words are often the best.

Mangosuthu Buthelezi

Life has taught me that what is important is service. That the journey on this Earth in life is a mixture of sweet and bitter, and that we also suffer. I always take encouragement as a Christian from the scriptures. Christ himself says that whosoever follows me must have his cross before him. I find it very strengthening when I falter and I feel my powers flag. Without pain how can one know the opposite of pain?

Richard Dawkins

Mostly, since I am a biologist, life has taught me what it is, where it comes from, and why it exists.

Zac Goldsmith

Above all, life has taught me that within the human animal lies the very best and the very worst. Our ancestors believed in something larger than the human. They held their ancestors as guardians of the moral code, or they worshipped different characteristics of the natural world. Or they believed in the overwhelming power of the Almighty. Today our leaders believe in nothing larger than the human itself. They believe we inherited a malformed Earth, and that it is our job to restructure it. They believe essentially that God did a bad job. This has developed into an obsession with technological and scientific "progress," and lunatic ideas of inhabiting other planets once ours has been bled dry. According to Neil Armstrong, the prime benefit of reaching the moon was the lesson that man must no longer feel duty-bound to remain "chained to this Earth."

The same techno-obsessed logic has been applied across the board. Nuclear power, for instance, was applied before anyone had developed a safe means of handling the inevitable radioactive waste. This apparently was of no concern to the scientists who claimed that by the time such waste was generated, science would have found the solution. Science never found that solution, and the result has been that large areas of the planet are radioactive. Because man is God, in their eyes, we can do no wrong. If we are to move ahead, it will be through restoring to humanity a feeling of deference toward the natural world. Restoring, too, the feeling that we are but one tiny part of a very large and complex system.

"I've found out that everything in the world is perfect, and that God knows what he's doing even though we don't."

STEVE VAI

His Holiness The Dalai Lama

When I am alive, I should utilize my energy, my existence, for good, for the benefit of others. That's important. Then I'm finished. Whether people say good things or bad things doesn't matter . . . When I reach Nirvana, then I will tell everything!

At the moment we are blessed with human life and with all the possibilities that this implies. Unlike animals and lower life forms, we are able to pluck the fruit of enlightenment, an act of ultimate goodness to both ourselves and others. However, death is pressing upon us from every side, threatening to rob us of this precious opportunity at any moment, and when we die nothing can be taken with us but the seeds of our life's work and our spiritual knowledge.

Shimon Peres

The lesson of life is that it is extremely short, so don't waste it on pessimism and disillusionment, on anger, it's a waste of time. Since it is so short, look upon it as flowers, not thorns: there is a taste and a smell and a form. I know that life always hits you and bites you, but I am grateful and I don't complain. By and large I was given many opportunities in my life, maybe more than I deserve, and I was encouraged and helped by so many people selflessly, for no reason. They never asked for anything in return.

Una M. Kroll

I have learned that life is full of suffering and joy. Neither is complete without the other. God is beyond both suffering and joy, and God sustains me in faith and love and hope. My teacher in all this is the person of Christ.

"Life has taught me that it's a wonderful adventure."

PETER USTINOV

Peter Ustinov

Life has taught me that it's a wonderful adventure. I've been married three times, but had I been married to my present wife initially I would have only been married once. That's very easy to say, but at the same time I may not have had the same children, which I would greatly regret. There are an enormous number of paradoxes and contradictions in life, and I think that life would be poorer without them. One may dream of perfection, only to find it is not worth having because perfection in itself is death, perfection is motionless and colorless. You can't have personality and be perfect at the same time.

Seyyed Hossein Nasr

What life has taught me essentially is that the supreme goal of life is to know the truth and to live by the truth. That, I would say, is the greatest lesson that life has taught me. I have suffered a great deal several times in my life, most of all during the Iranian revolution when I lost all of my property, my belongings, my house, and my private library. I had to start my life from ground zero in 1979. When I came out of Iran with my wife and two children, it was an extremely traumatic experience, but I was able to transcend all of that, because for me the life of the world was not really life. What life really was, was my immersion in knowledge of the truth. By knowledge I mean real wisdom, *jnana* in Sanskrit, the knowledge of salvation. I came to understand very early the meaning of the life of this world as a test, as the Qur'an says. Life most of the time is a trial; it is there to test us.

Gore Vidal

Life's taught me nothing I didn't know going in. It is unjust and that is to be expected. Most people collapse under injustice or conform. I was born to be a fighter, a very Gore characteristic, so I have been fulfilled by life. Life has given me so much injustice, not only personal but also in the world around me. So I always have adrenaline flowing; I always have a sharp knife.

Jilly Cooper

Life so far has taught me that you learn absolutely nothing by experience. I think the only way to cope with a terrible disaster in your life is to hope it will make you more compassionate and able to help people in similar situations.

Ed Begley Jr.

Life's taught me to live simply. To take what I need, which turns out to be a lot less than I thought I needed when I was a teenager. I wanted a big house and a hot tub and a fast car. Then at a fairly early age, about 20, I just tried to go in a different direction. I live in a very small, modest house; it's quite grand, though, on the global scale. There are people in most parts of the world that would regard this as a mansion and that's what I regard it as, it's the entire mansion I need. It's easy for me to do that as my father was a blue-collar fellow who made it later in life, so he lived in a similar house. I've always lived in a fairly simple place. I have everything I need and my needs have been met for many years.

David Lynch

Somewhere along the line, life taught me to see that there is quite a beautiful future for us, every human being. They say we are sparks of the divine flame. Having the potential to see the big picture and to live the big picture is in every person.

Sharon Stone

Life teaches you to pick yourself up, dust yourself down, and start all over again.

Anjelica Huston

Life has taught me that you have to confront things and not shy away from them. I don't like to go to the doctors; I am scared of what they are going to tell me, yet they are there for the benefit of my health and well-being. I've learned that it's good for me to brave that out once in a while, and not fall prey to my fears. Fear and excitement run very close to me, I think it is part of my makeup and probably why I am naturally attracted to acting. The feeling of heightened adrenaline.

"Life has taught me that it's the hardest thing you can do."

BOB GELDOF

QUESTION

7

What advice or words of wisdom would you like to pass on to those close to you?

Nelson Mandela

The values of yesterday are not the values of today, so one has to be very careful about giving advice, to young people in particular. You know my son came to see me in jail, when he turned 16, and I thought it was my duty to talk to him and tell him how to behave. I thought he was listening very carefully. When I finished he laughed and he said, "Dad, don't give me unsolicited advice, if I want advice from you I will ask you. Moreover, what you have told me is old hat, it no longer applies." So I am very careful about giving advice.

"Life is tough; you have to believe in yourself."

ILANA GOOR

Ilana Goor

Don't be afraid of life and don't be afraid to try. If you want something, go after it, nobody is going to help you but yourself. Some people will help you if they see that you are trying, but don't expect anything from anybody, because if you expect, you get disappointed. If you can give, give. Find somebody that you can share with, because if you don't have somebody to share with it's not worthwhile. You have to share your happiness, your sadness, with someone you trust. Don't bother other people with your anxiety, with your sadness, with your diseases, because they don't like it. People always go where they see the light. Come to people with happy thoughts. If you get a gift, be happy because it's very rare, accept it, and don't say, "No, I don't need it." Accept it because if they give it to you, they want to give it to you. Life is tough; you have to believe in yourself. This is not something you can teach somebody. People can encourage you, the ones who love you and are your friends; but at the end of the day you are born alone and you are going to die alone.

Gore Vidal

I don't advise. I think that if you have led your life properly, you've made an example—in my case over three-quarters of a century. I am hated in many quarters and loved in many quarters. I tell the truth, because I'm on the people's side. It is responding to injustice, responding to stupidity, which thrills and energizes me. I'm never more pleased. So, my advice is my life. You can look at it from one direction and say, "Oh God, what a disaster." Or you can look at it from another and say, "He did it his way."

Michael Fitzpatrick

Dream. Dream all the time. Dream of what was and what is to come. Take action. Initiate, plan and follow through. Remain committed at all times. Laugh as hard as you can.

Bono

I wouldn't say it's advice but to the people close to me I would say that I wish I listened to you more.

Albina du Boisrouvray

When you want to help people and feel overwhelmed by the scale of what needs to be done, think of the starfish story, which is a great booster of courage. It's the story of a man on a beach covered with stranded and dying starfish who sees a woman taking them one by one and throwing them back into the ocean. He says to her, "Why are you doing all this? There are millions of starfish and the beach goes on for miles and you just cannot put them all back into the ocean, so what does it matter?" She has one in her hand and she throws it into the water to give it back its life and says, "It matters completely to this one, so it's this one that counts."

Alfredo Guevara

For my words to be wise, I would have to be a wise man. That is not my profession. But I would advise others to do what they can to cherish their humanity, their human qualities. And humanity is, above all, a matter of nurturing one's capacity to get into other peoples' skin in order to understand them.

Peter Ustinov

Examine everything you are told before reacting to it, and then, after you have thought about it a long time, think again.

Michael Radford

To my son, I would say that life is three things. It is a materialistic existence, there is no point in denying it, because if you deny that you deny a part of life. But it's also a spiritual existence; whichever way you want to look at it, it is an immense mystery. You just have to stand and look at the sky at night, which I do on a regular basis, to understand that we know nothing, we know nothing of our ultimate destiny, we know nothing about anything. The distances between the stars and the infinity of the universe, the black holes, the collapsing and fading of stars, the birth of stars, I look at that and I think, my God, you have to understand the spiritual nature of the universe. Thirdly, you have to understand the extraordinary gift of human creativity. Every single person has a creative quality in them and unless you use it on a regular basis you stagnate. You must live every day of your life because it is not for wasting.

Zac Goldsmith

If I could pass on one thread of a message, it would be simply that God has done a very good job with the world. We should learn to love it. Rather than engaging in battle with our surroundings in an attempt to adapt them to our needs, I sincerely believe we must seek to adapt ourselves to the world's needs.

Gianfranco Ferre

Be true to yourself, and try to be as correct toward others as possible.

> "Believe in your own experience, dare to be alive, dare to do what you believe is your destiny."
>
> PAULO COELHO

Paulo Coelho

Believe in your own experience, dare to be alive, dare to do what you believe is your destiny. Rely on the experience of other people, but not on the wisdom of other people, because it is useless. Don't try to accumulate knowledge. You can be a very cultivated person but you cannot carry this into your next life, so try to be open to the mysteries of life. Wisdom is experience, and being able to live in constant communion with God. I have studied the so-called occult world, the so-called religious world, all my life and I end up realizing that maybe even the simplest person, who didn't have to read the encyclopedia of religion and the occult, is closer to God than I am. So rely on the example of other people but try to give yourself your own chance and be an example. Live your own experience because it is unique.

Frei Betto

Do not try to seize the water of the river. It always looks the same, but it constantly renovates itself. Do not try to alter the banks of the river. Just struggle to keep the water clean and build bridges between the banks.

Anjelica Huston

Care for your loved ones. Eat healthy food, think healthy thoughts. Spend time in nature. Try to get a good night's sleep. Try not to ponder the future too much or the past too much, stay with the present, see how you get along moment to moment. Follow your dream. Express yourself.

Shimon Peres

My advice would be to take yourself seriously and to remember that your potential is much greater than you think. Try always to mobilize from within yourself talents that are suppressed or hidden, and bring them to use. But be careful that your ego doesn't become greater than yourself. Build on your potential, not your ego.

Farah Pahlavi

To never lose hope and to count your blessings. Also, to sharpen your five senses, to think positively, to be loving and compassionate, to find and appreciate beauty, be it in nature, music, literature, or friendship. One has to use every means possible to feel at peace with oneself. I believe very much in sports and meditation.

Mangosuthu Buthelezi

My advice would be to remember that as human beings we are not created perfect. To get to that state of perfection, which we think our Lord and our mentors would wish us to reach, is a constant struggle that we will always be engaged in to the end of our days. I would also say that the great thing is to serve. The biggest accomplishment one can attain on this Earth is being a servant, obedient to God.

Charles Le Gai Eaton

Advice depends entirely upon the person concerned and their circumstances, bearing in mind that those who ask for it usually seek only confirmation of the course they have already chosen. When I was young I was deluged with so much bad advice that I hesitate to advise!

Robert Fisk

I think my advice to journalists would be that you should challenge your authorities, especially when they are at war, challenge your army as well as their army, and challenge your side's lies as well as the other side's lies. It's even more important to do it in time of war than in time of peace. The rallying call to be patriotic and support the boys and therefore shut up in war is wrong. I think many of my colleagues work with the centers of power, they don't monitor them.

Amos Gitai

I would say to people working in cinema, just try and find a way to believe in what you do, and articulate it. In the kind of films I make, I would like the viewer to enter into some sort of exchange and to try to interpret them, because I think it is a mistake to spell out everything, and to spoon-feed people. You have to provoke them to some extent, but also to let them read what signals you are giving them. I think that's an interesting exchange.

Richard Dawkins

I would say to people you are fantastically privileged to be alive. Make use of the eyes that you have been given, the ears that you have been given, the brain that you have been given, the hands that you have been given, to discover, to apprehend, to understand as much as you possibly can before you die; about why you were ever born in the first place; and about the place in which you find yourself. And while you are here, do all in your power to leave the world a better place than you found it.

Sharon Stone

Remember that your whole life is just this minute. This is your life, so live widely and fully and plenteously, in the now.

Harry Dean Stanton

Wisdom is to realize that we are nothing, just part of the manifestation of this whole universe, and that we go back into nothing. Relax, be quiet, be still. Surrender to what is.

Dadi Janki with Sister Jayanti

Try to be detached from the influence of the world and to be loved by God. These are my good feelings for those close to me. I keep whispering these secrets all the time.

David Lynch

There are many roads that lead to Rome, so it is tricky giving advice or recommending things. People need to become seekers and expand their own awareness. Along with this awareness and consciousness come so many positive things, that life just seems to get better and better.

Seyyed Hossein Nasr

I would say to always remain truthful to one's true self and to try to know oneself in depth. The famous Delphic saying, "Know thyself," is the key. By "self" is not meant the ego, but most of all the supreme Spirit that resides within us and that emanates through all of being. Ultimately to know oneself is to know God, as the Prophet said. To remain true to oneself is also to remain true to one's vocation in the world, to one's function in this earthly life. It is to remain sincere and truthful in all the other relationships that we experience in this world, with other human beings, with even the nonhuman world, and, of course, most of all with God. That is my supreme advice.

Emma Sergeant

My advice is to be humble, be grateful, otherwise what's the point of trying for anything when you can never console yourself with the small things of life? One of the great joys in my life is to go off and do stupid things like going shopping, because I feel so grateful that I can go and spend money, that I can go and do something really silly. I can meet people in the street and chat and live in one of the most wonderful cities in the world, and live in the best area, and be paid for what I love doing. God, what else can I ask for, except health? All these people who sit there counting all the things they don't have, is just mind-blowing to me. So just be grateful and be humble.

Sophia Loren

I would like to pass on to those close to me only one piece of advice: be honest in and with yourself.

"My suggestion or advice is very simple; that is, to have a sincere heart."

HIS HOLINESS THE DALAI LAMA

His Holiness The Dalai Lama

As human beings we have good qualities as well as bad ones. Now, anger, attachment, jealousy, hatred, are the bad side; these are the real enemy. From a certain point of view, our real enemy, the real troublemaker, is inside. So these bad thoughts remain active, as long as you have these, it is difficult to attain a mental peace . . . My suggestion or advice is very simple; that is, to have a sincere heart.

Jools Holland

I wouldn't presume to advise those close to me because I think they'd find it a bit annoying. One of the things I do say to people is that in music one of the important things is to love the music itself and to enjoy the music. Doing it to get money out of it is something completely different.

Steve Vai

If you're looking for life-advice or precious words of wisdom, then seek the words and/or writings of truly inspired people whose spiritual evolution is supreme. They, and only they, have the authority to proclaim actual words of wisdom that should be accepted. Now, if you wanted to know how to play a song on the guitar, forget those guys, I can show you that.

Bob Geldof

I'm not very good at life, as life appears to me to be very hard, so what words of wisdom or clues do I have to pass on? A couple of mates of mine are Falstaffian in their embrace of life, they view it as a monstrous hoot. They do everything to the max, everything. Right out there risking everything in business, drink, drugs, women, love, children, sport, all to the max. It's refreshing for me to be around them, it makes me see things through their eyes for a change. It's not in my makeup. I'd panic if I lived right out there, on that edge. I'd fear poverty and loneliness too much.

"Only love can overcome evil in the end."

UNA M. KROLL

Una M. Kroll

Christ's teaching in Matthew 22.32–40 is that if you truly love God, you will only do what pleases God and what pleases God is to love God with all your heart and soul and mind and to love your neighbor as yourself. My whole life is based upon the principle of resistance to evil through nonviolent means and through not paying back evil in kind. That adds to the total sum of evil in the world. Only love can overcome evil in the end.

Jilly Cooper

My favorite words of wisdom are attributed to a Quaker missionary, Stephen Grellet, who was born in France in the 18th century and worked in America: "I expect to pass through this world but once. Any good thing, therefore, that I can do or any kindness that I can show to any fellow creature, let me do it now. Let me not defer or neglect it, for I shall not pass this way again."

Jack Nicholson

I am not a great giver of advice. But as a parent, you hope that your influence would be a positive one. Do good work, harm no other person . . . all of those things. I am a pretty good coach of the immediate. I have an arsenal for this, but there are times even with your children when you know you can't say anything. Never give someone your best advice because they won't follow it.

Ed Begley Jr.

Just slow down. In the pursuit of even the highest, the loftiest goals, we sometimes rush so much. There's a true story about a friend of mine who made elaborate travel arrangements to meet a guru at the Temple of Tranquillity in Indonesia. Things went wrong with his travel plans, he missed connections, got delayed, and had to make other complicated plans to get there. He finally arrived in Indonesia, hired a car to take him to the temple, and said to the driver, "The Temple of Tranquillity and step on it!" The driver started to laugh and my friend started to laugh. That's what we do, even with the highest goals. We say, "I want serenity and I want it now, dammit!"

"Just slow down."

ED BEGLEY JR.

QUESTION

8

Do you believe our survival on planet Earth is being threatened?

David Frost

There are two entirely conflicting responses to the idea that our survival is threatened in terms of environment and global warming and all the rest. The first is that there are chilling warnings from people who should know, and they are very well worth listening to. That has to be balanced against a second response. Going back to the early '70s, Dr. Paul Ehrlich, who was one of the great gurus of the young in America, made shattering predictions as to what was going to happen to the planet. In fact his warnings of doom and destruction have not happened. I think there is a sense in which we as a people do tend to prevail in the end, even if it may be very near the brink. For instance, in the early '50s the air here in London was full of smog, people were dying of bronchitis and so on, and then a Clean Air Act was passed, which solved that problem. There is no smog in London now. So I think the human being does tend, maybe at the last minute, to allow common sense to come through. It's a balance of those two things.

"If you poison the river, the river will poison you: wherever you want to go in the Third World, you will find they all know that."

GORE VIDAL

Gore Vidal

Of course our survival on the planet is being threatened. I would be very surprised if the human race was here in a century. I think that we are essentially suicidal and this shows up in the inability to gauge cause and effect. If you poison the river, the river will poison you: wherever you want to go in the Third World, you will find they all know that. They don't poison their drinking supply. We do because there is money in it. So we are wrecking the planet and we all know we are, but it does not suit our rulers to do anything about it while money is being made. It is my own example and that of others to counteract this. Will we win? I don't think so. There are too many people here now. There will be a great dying out, and unless we can manage to take our infection to another planet we will use this one up.

Dadi Janki with Sister Jayanti

I believe that we will come out of the present situation of upheaval and breakdown, because God is eternal, the spirit is eternal, and civilization cannot just finish and end. The things that are happening today are teaching us many lessons, and humanity as a whole will learn these lessons. The pain that is coming to us through the circumstances of the world is making us aware of the dimension of values and spirituality. So a powerful and growing minority today are coming to that new consciousness. I think there is definitely a golden age ahead of us.

Anjelica Huston

I feel that we are looking at a particularly cynical time in terms of how we take for granted all the amazing benefits of nature. Poisoning the seas and darkening the skies: it is an ongoing source of amazement to me that people seem so oblivious of what they are doing to their environment. Small things do make a difference, and I feel if you can instill that idea in people, you can make a difference. Try to leave the place a little nicer than you found it, plant a tree, do something, pick up a piece of garbage. It would make a huge difference.

Zac Goldsmith

I don't believe we will survive on this planet for more than a few decades unless we divert dramatically from our current path. I do not believe the god of technology can save us. On the contrary, I believe our faith in technological change will hasten this unnecessary destruction. We can, without too much difficulty, reverse these depressing trends, but we can only do so with the will of political leadership, and this is increasingly corrupt.

Robert Fisk

Clearly nuclear weapons are a threat in anyone's hands. But I'm very much against the idea of survival on the planet being the great issue. It's a nice rallying call for people who are worried about the environment and Kyoto, and they should be concerned about it. But the planet will carry on. I'm sure waste heaps and detritus will get ever larger, and dangerous nuclear power stations will eventually be closed down. But look at what previous generations went through, look at how whole societies were wiped out by the Black Death. The events of September 11, 2001, an international crime against humanity, did not change the world in that way. But its spectacular nature has allowed it to become the turning point for ruthless men and women to persuade gullible people that they should live a life of fear. There was that lovely phrase from *A Man for All Seasons:* "These are tales to frighten children, Master Secretary."

"If we want a beautiful garden, we must first have a blueprint in the imagination, a vision."

HIS HOLINESS THE DALAI LAMA

His Holiness The Dalai Lama

In the case of such global issues as the conservation of the earth, and indeed in taking all problems, the human mind is the key factor. Whether they are problems of economics, international relations, science, technology, medicine or ecology, though these issues seem to be beyond any one individual's capacity, where the problem begins and where the answer must first be sought is within. In order to change the external situation we must first change within ourselves. If we want a beautiful garden, we must first have a blueprint in the imagination, a vision. Then that idea can be implemented and the external garden can be materialized.

Charles Le Gai Eaton

Yes, of course our survival is being threatened. We always want "more and more" (as the Qur'an warned us) and if we are allowed that "more and more" (which is what technology offers), ignoring all natural limits, we are on the path of destruction. The Islamic perspective implies that God gives us enough rope to hang ourselves. The Qur'an frequently speaks of generations—nations or tribes—who were destroyed because they had lost the sense of the sacred and because they had ventured too far beyond the limits set for us and brought destruction upon themselves. A point comes when God says, in effect, "Enough is enough." We may now be near that point. But, in talking about the environment we are isolating one symptom of the sickness: the decline of spirituality, of the sense of the sacred, of awareness of the symbolism inherent in the natural world—these things all go together.

Paulo Coelho

No, I don't believe our survival is threatened. I believe that we cannot destroy what God created, we don't have this power. Only God could decide to reshape the whole thing and give us power to destroy ourselves. He can use us to reshape this whole situation.

Michael Radford

I think that as long as we can say that human life on this planet is threatened, we are safe. So far in history, we've had a capacity to understand the threats. Good and bad are somehow counter-balanced. We are horribly threatened, and yet it may just be that eventually the way into the future is that we will be able to duplicate nature. I certainly think it is only a matter of time before we control both birth and death. It may be frightening because we don't have the philosophical tools to deal with it. But philosophy and morals are catching up, and, curiously, they catch up on a very day-to-day level, as with the debate on cloning. We are under threat from things we possibly don't know about at this particular moment. It may well be that these threats overbalance and tip us into catastrophe. And it may just be that the human race is doomed for extinction anyway.

Peter Ustinov

I think it's very good for us to think of our survival being threatened because it wakes us up to all sorts of terrible possibilities. Nothing in the planetary system is permanent.

Alfredo Guevara

I believe there's an urgent need on the part of politicians and decision-makers to think about what is happening to human life on our planet, interiorize, and question themselves in a climate of personal serenity. If they don't, we will continue on this frantic, insane course, following false paths that are self-destructive. The human race, with all the richness and spiritual experience it has accumulated, could perish. All this comes from an inversion of our scale of values, which has made noise and banality rule. And when I say noise, I mean noise in the soul.

Michael Fitzpatrick

Yes, the threat to our survival is not immediate, but the signs are everywhere. We must bring the world back into balance before it is too late. All of us must work together to do this.

Jools Holland

I think there have always been risks to our survival. The fact that there are more people now than there ever have been, and that people have great weapons, is a rather frightening thought. But I don't think we're necessarily headed for immediate disaster.

Seyyed Hossein Nasr

Our survival is being threatened directly by the wedding between power created through technology and human passions that are growing wild without spiritual control. This conjunction was the invention of modern civilization, which created a science based on power rather than wisdom. So human beings have gained greater possibilities for destruction, but in terms of controlling their passions they have not even remained on the same level as men and women of old. Greed was once a sin. Today it is considered a virtue, and modern man sets no limits on what he can do with his power. Modern life is based on tremendous hubris, creating a situation where for the first time the life of the whole planet is threatened. Unfortunately, very few people want to face the deeper causes that have brought about the present crisis. When I spoke about the ecological crisis in the 1960s, no theologian in England was interested in listening. At that time, many Western theologians and historians thought it was the teachings of Christianity that had created modern science and technology and took great pride in this matter. Forty years later few speak in this way anymore because the crisis caused by the application of modern technology has become so great. But few people want to talk about the responsibility of modern science and technology because everyone thinks that the solution will come through the application of the very factors that created the problem in the first place. We are destroying the rule of life globally because we have lost the sacred view of nature, which was rooted in religion. As long as there is not that awakening, the danger remains very great.

> "We are destroying the rule of life globally because we have lost the sacred view of nature, which was rooted in religion."
>
> SEYYED HOSSEIN NASR

Sophia Loren

The big threat in the world today is the disparity between rich and poor, between people who are well nourished and people who are starving. As long as this situation continues there will always be conflicts, wars, and other risks to human survival on this planet.

Una M. Kroll

Yes, I believe that we are destroying our planet through exploitation of nature, pollution, and carelessness faster than we can achieve it through nuclear weapons. After the pursuit of peace this care for our environment is the most important focus in my prayer and life. I look, even at my age, to ways of making this known to people I come into contact with, and I look actively for allies.

Jack Nicholson

I don't feel our survival is threatened in the immediate sense. But I think the fragmented nature of modern life, with these talks about stem-cell research and so on, keeps us underinformed about the real issues. If survival is the goal of science, then we are very shortsighted in our planning.

David Lynch

There are a lot of screwball things going on that are really harmful to human beings and the planet. That's all the more reason to try to get in tune with nature, the natural laws. Live in tune with things rather than go against them.

Amos Gitai

Yes, I think people won't take the measures to protect the planet, and they will just destroy the entire planet and there will be nothing left. I think that is a real danger because humanity, unfortunately, is not extremely intelligent and people learn only when they get hit over the head. Until then, they don't stop, and it's a very bad way of learning.

Farah Pahlavi

I do not think we will be threatened to the point of extinction, but we are creating a great many problems. Since I always want to think positively, I hope that there will be enough wise people in the world who will see what we are doing to our planet, the environment, and to the survival of mankind. We are so bound to each other that the problem of one area can affect the rest of the world. We cannot live separately.

Harry Dean Stanton

The sun is burning out—eventually it's going to go. Saving the world—for what, you know? That doesn't mean that you don't try to keep the air clean and clean up your house while you are here, clean up the planet, do what you can, but again that is preordained also. Some people will do it, others won't. So, be still, and do nothing, and see what happens.

Jilly Cooper

I think life on the planet is horrendously threatened by commercialism on the rampage. The rainforests crash, the Arctic Circle is melting, the world is warming, and none of the big nations seems to be taking this seriously. Also, with rogue nations and powerful nations armed to the teeth, how much longer will it be before somebody launches a nuclear bomb? So I fear for our lovely planet. I'd love everybody to go to the moon so they could look back at the planet Earth and realize how beautiful it is, and how we need to cherish it, and look after it every moment of our lives.

"With people killing each other in the name of land and religion, the planet probably has a better chance without us."

BOB GELDOF

Bob Geldof

The planet will survive without a problem. Humans will pass on and die out as a species, I think. There will probably be some shifts and change just like there always have been in the past, whether it is another ice age or something else. Evolution will continue: it will just sidestep and go off and find another path. Evolution will find a means of instilling intelligence into whatever future creatures there will be. With people killing each other in the name of land and religion, the planet probably has a better chance without us. We must all take a major step to change these things.

Richard Dawkins

In terms of a survival that is worth having, yes we are certainly threatened—by the danger of overpopulation in the long run, and by destruction of the environment in which we live. I do feel passionately about the destruction of wild places such as the rainforests, and of wild creatures such as elephants and rhinos—forms that have taken hundreds and millions of years to evolve and which can be destroyed. Ecosystems such as the rainforests are being destroyed daily by commercial interests. These things don't by themselves threaten our survival in the short term, but added up over the long term they could. I do not see any danger or threat to humanity coming from genetic experimentation, for example, on organisms. I think it's a case of newspapers crying wolf. I worry more about the overuse of antibiotics.

Albina du Boisrouvray

We have for sure done things that threaten the survival of the planet. We need to put more love and respect into the attitude we have toward this miracle that we are so privileged to live on. Let's hope that nature is sufficiently vast and strong that it will somehow compensate, maybe at the expense of humans and their greediness—who knows?

Robert Graham

Yes, we are threatened. I think that from one point of view this kind of political correctness about the Earth is good because the greatest polluters are America and the European countries. On the other hand, the less industrialized Third World countries have not had much chance to pollute anything, so you're taking away their chance to pollute, which is in some way an extreme kind of racism, a backward form of exploitation.

Ed Begley Jr.

I think we will survive but it will be like people survive in a bunker, it's not much of a life. It'll be like the worst that *Blade Runner* had to prophesy, a kind of apocalyptic *Mad Max* vision. What will remain intact years hence if we continue on this path, just like spoiled children eating everything at the party? If global warming causes sea levels to rise precipitously, it could be a real problem for the survival of some people—in Bangladesh, for example—who would be inundated. The more affluent nations will find higher ground, and they'll do fine. But what kind of life is it when you see so many people perish around you, and it becomes the "I'm aboard the lifeboat, pull up the ladder" mentality that you see so much of today?

Steve Vai

I think the world is like a big washing machine and in the big picture it survives our abuse. Our abuse of the planet will only result in our own extinction until the planet cleans itself up and we reincarnate back to evolve some more. In this scenario our survival is not threatened, if you are talking about the soul. If you are referring to the physical, then yes, we are blowing ourselves out of the water.

Bono

The Armageddon scenario is probably a little less of a threat than it was 25 years ago, but we still live in a world where mutually assured destruction is seen as a solution to problems, and I think that is ridiculous.

Nelson Mandela

Scientists keep on alarming us. They recently talked of a very heavy asteroid, which they thought was going to hit part of the Earth, and said that it would destroy a large number of people, as an earlier asteroid destroyed the dinosaurs. But now some other scientists say that this asteroid will miss the Earth. So that is a relief.

Mangosuthu Buthelezi

I always believed in conservation, even before it was fashionable. It is God's plan that we should respect the Earth. As we advance we have to have progress, but at what price?

"It is God's plan that we should respect the Earth."

MANGOSUTHU BUTHELEZI

Shimon Peres

I think if there is a Lord in heaven His main task is balancing opposing force—danger and hope, life and death—because otherwise we would have disappeared a long time ago. And you know the Lord was dissatisfied with what He did when He first created the world, in seven days according to the Jewish tradition. He had a good look and didn't like it. He brought on a flood. He has tried to improve it endlessly, yet it goes on as a story of contradictory forces. In the annals of humankind, if there is a danger of destruction there are also forces of maintenance. A fire brigade.

QUESTION

9

Who do you most admire in this world, historical or living?

Henry Dean Stanton

Gandhi. There is no other human being who has lived on this planet who did what he did. He defeated a whole country without raising a hand. Christ, of course, and Buddha were great souls, but Gandhi put in action what Christ and Buddha were talking about. I have never found any incident in history like that. So he would be the greatest influence. I think it was Einstein who said Gandhi put his life on the line—and eventually was killed for it, just like Christ was killed.

Bono

The person I most admire is Jesus Christ.

Bob Geldof

I admire lots of anonymous individuals I've met for the things they've done and the way they have chosen to live their lives. From the past, the person I feel affection for is Samuel Pepys because he strikes me as being eminently human, and he achieved a lot coming from nothing. That was important for him and he was always impressed by himself. He was so curious about life and other people, and embraced all that and wanted to learn, and noted his own foibles, and had a great relationship with his wife. I am fond of him and admire him as a historical character.

In our time, the one you stand in awe of is Nelson Mandela. Never mind his huge bravery, intelligence, integrity, and moral courage, which you shrink in front of. How many of us would be prepared to sit in jail for life for what they believed in? Beyond all that, he is an amazing person; a great boxer in his youth; adores pretty girls; falls in love with any pretty girl he sees, he is hugely charming, so eloquent, and wears the worst shirts you've ever seen in your life but thinks they're great. Some of the things he says I profoundly disagree with, but you can argue the toss with him, which is great. And he doesn't stand on dignity, though he is hugely dignified. What he is is an Edwardian gentleman; and kind. A great man.

Nelson Mandela

There is no individual that I admire. But all those who are deeply concerned about poverty, who want to help to get humanity out of poverty. Those are my heroes, whoever they are.

Gianfranco Ferre

I admire people who have helped people to express themselves in ways such as painting or writing, inventors like the printer Johannes Gutenberg, for example. Also people who invented medicines. Mostly I admire people who helped humanity to develop.

Ed Begley Jr.

Henry David Thoreau was a wonderful man who taught us a lot. I'm also a fan of Rachel Carson who wrote *Silent Spring* and taught us about the damage caused by pesticides—what had already happened and what she felt would happen. Even though they tried to negate her theories and ridicule her book, enough people had seen problems with dying birds and thin-shelled, deformed eggs that wouldn't hatch to think she was right. So they banned DDT. I think people will do good if faced with an environmental situation that's undeniably real.

Farah Pahlavi

During my extensive travels throughout Iran and across the world, I have come to meet ordinary people who have been a source of inspiration for me, because of their dignity and "grandeur d'âme." Among historical figures, I admire Cyrus the Great (590–529 BC). His edict in Babylon known as Cyrus's Cylinder (British Museum) is the earliest declaration of human rights: "I ordered that all should be free to worship their god without harm, I ordered that no one's home be destroyed and no one's property be looted. I ordered all closed places of worship, which were built in ancient times, to be reopened. I brought their people together and rebuilt their homes and restored peace and tranquillity for all."

I also admire great composers, writers—especially the famous poets of Iran such as Ferdowsi, Rumi, Omar Khayam,

Hafez, and Saadi—and our scientist Avicenna. I admire the founder of modern Iran, Reza Shah the Great, and my late husband, Mohammad Reza Shah Pahlavi, who continued his father's legacy into modernity, especially in establishing a civil code of justice and education, working for the emancipation of women, and securing the territorial integrity of Iran. Abraham Lincoln, Mahatma Gandhi, General Charles de Gaulle are among my other favorite statesmen.

Sophia Loren

For me, one man stands out above all: Gandhi.

> "I admire above all those people who have demonstrated a willingness to rethink basic assumptions."
>
> ZAC GOLDSMITH

Zac Goldsmith

An easier question is which people I least admire. Here the list is long and the reasons many. But those I admire, besides members of my own family, include Mahatma Gandhi. He presented a worldview that we would do well to observe. He understood the problems of scale. He understood the importance of the natural world, of the need for cultural identity. Living today, I admire above all those people who have demonstrated a willingness to rethink basic assumptions. Nuclear physicists who have admitted the problems associated with their work. World Bank executives who have blown the whistle on that questionable institution. Politicians who have accepted responsibility for bad decisions. These people are vital. Oscar Wilde once wrote that an intelligent man is one who agrees with you. If that is so, then Prince Charles would feature high on my list. He, more than virtually every other establishment figure, has displayed tremendous courage in addressing unfashionable issues like genetic engineering, modern architecture, and industrial agriculture.

Richard Dawkins

I admire Charles Darwin, for his intellectual contribution and because he was a model of a very, very decent, kind, humane human being as well.

Frei Betto

Francis of Assisi, friend of the poor, brother of nature, disciple of Jesus.

Michael Radford

Nelson Mandela is a man whose fortitude in the face of odds is quite an incredible symbol to the human race. And he has written wise things about everything, which is astonishing, and we are very lucky to be living in a world where he exists. But he has his failings as a human being, there is no question: I am sure that within his political structure he was a ruthless man. I admire William Shakespeare because I think, never mind what kind of man he was, to have that deep perception of the world both in poetry and in drama is absolutely unique. So, in terms of creativity, with that breadth and understanding, he would probably be the person I admire the most. In a way I don't admire any one person, but there are qualities such as physical and moral courage that I lack and find admirable in people. I think that people who do what they believe in actually are the people who I admire the most. The average modest, humble person who tries to lead a good life is to me often infinitely more heroic and admirable than politicians, leaders, generals, and people like that.

"Above all, I admire integrity."

ALFREDO GUEVARA

Alfredo Guevara

I wouldn't like to pick names. But I admire men and women who give their lives for the happiness of others. That is to say that, above all, I admire integrity. And, of course, among those who give their lives for others, I'm not only thinking of the heroes of liberation wars. I think a great deal about those writers who have managed to deepen the human soul and so transmit very valuable ideas to their contemporaries, and of the great scientists who have captured small spaces, because they are small, from the great mystery. Those are my Olympians.

Robert Graham

The continuum is what I admire. I can look at something that was made 2,000 years ago and understand it completely because I could have made it. I can only admire something if I see in it something that I can understand, such as a painting that I could have painted. So, it's not individuals like Shakespeare or Michelangelo that I admire. In a simpler time or a different age, I would have admired my master and I would have wanted to emulate him in molding my own entity, my own lump of clay.

David Frost

Apart from the obvious choice of Jesus Christ, a historical figure I admire is Cyrus the Great, because he was the first man to use power to enhance rather than degrade the human condition. In the world today I would pick Nelson Mandela. When I first interviewed him I asked, "How was it that you could be wrongly incarcerated for 28 years and still not be bitter, was it because of religion?" He said, "I would like to be bitter, but there is no time to be bitter, there is work to be done." Bill Clinton told me in an interview that he had called Nelson Mandela about two hours after he had walked to freedom and said, "I know you say you are not bitter, but as you walked out of that prison you must have hated the people who had put you there." Nelson Mandela replied, "No, I did not hate them, because if I hated them they would still be controlling me."

Jools Holland

I admire some people just because they are great artists and have made things that affect the soul. And other people because they are such spiritually great beings. One person who put the two things together is Solomon Burke, who is both a preacher and a singer. He has tremendous charm, one of the key things you need to succeed in music, which the Beatles and Duke Ellington had. I think that he gets that from being an incredibly gifted singer and also from his constant union with God. Something about him transcends his preaching and his music.

The Dalai Lama is rather great at what he does. If you think of all the awful things that have happened to him, he never complains about it. He just says very positive things all the time. Prince Charles is great because, like the Dalai Lama, he didn't choose his job, he just had it thrust upon him. And it's not the nicest job in the world always to be observed in everything you do. I think he does things because he genuinely cares about the world around him; there are a lot of people who in that position would just be a playboy or something else. I wouldn't want to think that I admire only famous people: I admire people who are stimulating to talk to.

Ilana Goor

Well, I admire innovative people who have the guts to change things. I admire some artists who started to do things before anybody else did. The artist I admire the most is Picasso. Not only because he was such a great artist, but also because he enjoyed life every day, he was extremely selfish and he did what he wanted to do. I admire those people who go against the stream, because it is so tough to do that. I admire Bell who invented the telephone, and the other inventors that people laughed at. The people who invented the plane, the Wright brothers. Those are the people who make the world go round.

"I admire innovative people who have the guts to change things."

ILANA GOOR

Charles Le Gai Eaton

The Prophet Muhammad. Beyond that—one person one week, another the next week, according to who is currently brought to my attention.

Dadi Janki with Sister Jayanti

Out of historical figures, I admire Mahatma Gandhi because of his spirit of renunciation and service. I also have a great deal of respect for Jesus Christ. Of people I have met, I have a lot of love for Nelson Mandela and for Mother Teresa (now a historical figure herself).

Albina du Boisrouvray

I admire people whose achievements I have witnessed myself, as with the historical you are never sure of the legend that created them. The person I admire most in the world is Nelson Mandela, that's for certain. I also admire people who have helped change things in people's lives directly, often when people have become victims of abuse to serve political and economic interests—Bernard Kouchner and the first French doctors of Médecins Sans Frontières, for example. In other fields, I admire the Romanian pianist Dinu Lipatti, who died in the 1940s. You only have to listen to his records and you can hear that he is a truly remarkable human being in the sense of an artist, like Maria Callas, someone else I deeply admire, a fantastic voice. If you admire people for who they are, you also admire what they have accomplished.

Anjelica Huston

Those I admire most are people like Stephen Hawking and Christopher Reeve, people with terrible life-threatening diseases and disabilities who strive on, and who have the extraordinary aptitude and courage to stay with the hand they've been dealt on Earth. People who survive battles and somehow transform them into something beautiful.

Robert Fisk

Must we always admire people? There aren't many Titans around at the moment, are there? I rather like Mohammed Khatami, the former president of Iran. I think he is basically a good person, one of the very few world leaders at the moment who is trustworthy on a personal and moral basis. He is a very thoughtful, very studious, and learned man. You don't often get learned people as leaders. Who is there in Europe we would really care to admire? War tends to throw up these titanic figures, whether they are of the extreme good or the extreme bad. Stalin, Hitler, Roosevelt, Churchill, Tito, de Gaulle, one might have loved or hated them but they were pretty extraordinary.

Since World War II, everyone would say our favorite South African prisoner, wouldn't they?—Nelson Mandela. He has become everyone's favorite leader, an iconic figure, who is ignored when he says uncharitable things about American policy in Iraq, but who we listen to carefully if he is talking about philosophy and so on. The two things are connected but we don't allow ourselves to think that. I admire people who go out of their way to try and do something they think is right and know they are going to suffer for it. Doctors in particular, people who work under fire. I knew a Norwegian doctor who was shot through the neck in Beirut and almost died. He was also shot in the liver in a gun battle, and he came back and kept on being a doctor. That's pretty brave.

> "I admire people who go out of their way to try and do something they think is right and know they are going to suffer for it."
>
> ROBERT FISK

SHIMON PERES

Moses and Ben-Gurion. One because of how I imagine him and the other because of the way I knew him. I am an Israeli and that is my tradition. Ben-Gurion was a genius with a fantastic memory, a strong character devoted to a cause, extremely courageous, and also daring, which is even more important than courage when you try to penetrate to new heights. I was his deputy and worked with him for 18 years, day in and day out. Every day was almost like a holiday, a very special day full of meaning, full of challenge.

Paulo Coelho

I most admire Nelson Mandela, a man I've never had a chance to meet. A man who was shaped by life itself, who never saw himself as a victim, a man who stands by his ideas, who doesn't care what others are thinking, and takes the steps he thinks are the correct ones. He is a man in the full sense of the word.

His Holiness The Dalai Lama

In past centuries, there have been many learned teachers who have laid down various paths to the realization of Truth. Among them, Lord Buddha is one, and my study of Buddhism has led me to form the opinion that, despite the differences in the names and forms used by the various religions, the ultimate truth to which they point is the same.

"I admire people who are dealing with the full deck, or striving to."

DAVID LYNCH

David Lynch

I admire people who are dealing with the full deck, or striving to. I admire and respect Maharishi Mahesh Yogi, because he has brought the beautiful teaching of transcendental meditation to anyone who wants it. It has brought a lot of help to a lot of people, and a way to expand consciousness and live life fully.

Seyyed Hossein Nasr

Historically, I admire most of all God's great messengers and prophets. The Prophet of Islam, Christ, Moses, Abraham, such great founders of other religions as Zoroaster, Buddha, Krishna, Lao-tsu, Confucius, and the great saints and seers of old. Of those living, I have great admiration and love for certain spiritual teachers, who have remained hidden but whom I have known. No one who is famous in the West is on the top of my list, but I admire some to a large degree. For example, I am a good friend of the Dalai Lama and have much respect for him. On the political level I have a great deal of respect for Prince Charles, whom I also know personally and whose views on friendship between religions, love for traditional art, the preservation of the animal world and the world of nature are very commendable. But the grandeur of human beings, let us say someone like Julius Caesar in Western history, is very hard to come by today.

Michael Fitzpatrick

Pablo Casals is, for me, the ultimate hero. His cello-playing career spanned White Houses from FDR to JFK. He lived to be 97 and was performing at his usual high energy level even then. He said, "Perhaps it is music that will save the world." He lived that proclamation in every note he played, every cause he championed and every protest he forged. "The cello is my oldest friend," he exclaimed. "All my life I have worked for peace."

Una M. Kroll

I would choose Jesus Christ, obviously, but I have been deeply influenced by Mahatma Gandhi, Martin Luther King, Helda Camera, and all those who strive to make peace without making war on their enemies. For this reason I admired a woman called Sadie Patterson, a Methodist who tried to do just that in Northern Ireland, and who is unknown outside her own circle. Also Julia de Beausobre, the author of *Creative Suffering,* whom I met twice when she was alive and who has had a profound influence on my life. She became for me the epitome of resistance in the Soviet Union in the 1920s and 1930s. Her husband was shot, her son died of starvation, and she was imprisoned, and then exiled. She devoted her life to prayer and making peace, wherever she was.

Mangosuthu Buthelezi

There are many people who I respect and admire. I would say that my mother was a very special person to me. I believe if there is any good in me it is because of her. Very often when I did something she admired, a speech or whatever, she would say, "Umfana wami" meaning "My boy" and my children would go out laughing, because they couldn't understand that this old man was her boy! My mother saw no age, and her love was unconditional.

Jack Nicholson

I am not a list-maker. If you are going to say Gandhi, why not say Jesus Christ? Or anybody who is making the full effort. Of my contemporaries, I admire a lot of people. Eleanor Roosevelt, Gloria who works for me. I sat here opposite John Huston and realized that at least for a short while I knew the best man alive. That is on a very personal level, it's not about what he did, it is just the actuality of the person.

Amos Gitai

I am very enthusiastic about people, about individuals, but I also think it's good to be a bit skeptical. I am not a sheer admirer. People will say Gandhi and so on, but the interesting thing about people is that they have contradictions, they are not perfect, and that's what makes them human. When they think they want to be perfect, they get into trouble. It is when they know how to coexist with their own contradiction that they become funny, nice and interesting.

Jilly Cooper

I hugely admire our Queen here, because she's brave, good, and has worked so hard to keep the Britain Royal Family going. I admire Winston Churchill because he had huge courage at a time when Britain was up against it during the war. Being a coward myself, I admire anyone who is prepared to suffer and die for their beliefs. I admire Beethoven for coping so bravely with adversity and writing the most marvelous music when he was going deaf. There must be an afterlife so artists like Schubert and Tchaikovsky can look down and realize how great and valuable their work really was. I also admire Emma Sergeant, because I think she is lovely and has exactly the right approach to art. She cheers everyone up and has such liveliness and guts to attack new things.

Emma Sergeant

Being an artist, Michelangelo, Leonardo da Vinci, I wish I could say them in the same breath. I think that, like Mozart, they just opened their hands and God poured all the gold dust possible into them. Those three for me are the greatest creatures that ever stalked the planet.

Gore Vidal

The human race exists, for me, to make me laugh. It makes me angry sometimes but it also makes me laugh. I would say I most admire the people who make me laugh the most.

QUESTION

10

How do you find peace within yourself?

Una M. Kroll

Peace found me when I was about five years old, at a time of unhappiness, and because it found me, I found it. For a long time now, I have been able to find peace through closing my eyes and imagining diving into a deep, cool pool of water, or using a similar image to help me to reach a stillness that is precious and refreshing. This is not prayer. I think it probably is a recourse to alpha waves, and once learned it is possible to reach that peace on request. But it does lead to prayer and, at times, to a sense of unity with creation. I consider it to be a gateway to prayer, to a kind of self-emptying. God enters that waiting space as the source of energy and abundant life, a spring of love welling up.

Nelson Mandela

My inner peace lies in the fact that I can serve the community. When I can serve the community I go to bed feeling satisfied that I have done something for the people.

Charles Le Gai Eaton

My inner peace lies in what Islam calls the Remembrance of God, specifically the *dhikr,* that is to say, invocation of the divine name. Outside that, it is impossible to be at peace in a "divided city," that is to say, amid the contradictions within myself, contrary impulses, troublesome memories, fantasies that never satisfy, distrust of my own body in old age. The French philosopher

Gustave Thibon has put it well: "In youth the body is our slave, in old age we are its slave." At this level, what is meant by peace? Freedom from worry about the current situation and about the future? Impossible. Contentment with oneself and with what one has done? Impossible. I am fairly cheerful by nature, but not at peace.

Frei Betto

Not considering insignificant events. I meditate every day, try to keep my sense of humor, and work for the downtrodden.

Bob Geldof

Find inner peace? I looked, it wasn't there. The only time I feel a sense of achievement or satisfaction is in music, largely when I play my songs, because then you are articulating your own psyche. There is a psychological catharsis and a physical relief, it is financially rewarding, and it's emotionally satisfying. So, if all those things are there, I sleep the sleep of the just, which I don't do very often. Off you go, free of all your nonsense. Again, writing a good song gives me a sense of satisfaction and achievement, even though everyone else may think it's crap. I like it and it fulfills a need in me, and when I hear it back it's like my psyche sending a postcard to itself.

"Find inner peace? I looked, it wasn't there."

BOB GELDOF

STEVE VAI

I mentioned the idea of asking ourselves to consider the spiritual consequence of any action before we perform it. When I am able to follow through with the healthy spiritual choice, that brings me a form of inner peace. There are many things that can bring momentary bliss in a mind filled with spinning whirlwinds, but the finest form of release comes from meditation. Sometimes it can be hell because you are confronted with the ceaseless meandering of the mind, but in those elusive moments where there is no thought, it's quite peaceful and fulfilling.

EMMA SERGEANT

My peace is to put my feet up on my table, light up a Gauloise Légère, and have a double espresso while looking at all the work I've done that day.

ALBINA DU BOISROUVRAY

You have to come to terms with what your life is, what it has been, what it has brought you, who you are, what the story is. And accept that it is, perhaps, not the story you thought it would be in the beginning. Coming to terms with all that and preserving a capacity for love helps me to find inner peace. Solitude brings me some inner peace too, moments of solitude. Nature, watching the ocean, and marveling at the seasons, the sun, the rain, the smell of the earth. Also reading and classical music, which sometimes brings me peace but is sometimes so beautiful that it is heartbreaking and takes you back into painful places. Listening to the mathematical harmony of Bach can soothe me and give me peace; harmony is something very important in life.

I think you probably feel more inner peace further down the road of your life than you do in the beginning or in the middle, before you have found your path. When you are not so full of anxiety, you can look back and think things are as they should be, and find peace.

"I am not looking for peace. I think life is confrontation."

PAULO COELHO

Paulo Coelho

I am not looking for peace. I think life is confrontation. Not in the sense of war but in the sense of movement.

I am closer to Jesus than to Buddha for example, I am closer to the idea that you have to face life and fight for changes within yourself, and every time you are changing you are not in peace, you are in confrontation with yourself. There are moments of peace and quiet, but then I am charging my batteries for the confrontation. If you read the *Bhagavad Gita,* when Arjuna goes to Krishna and says he is not going to fight and wants peace, Krishna says "No" to him. In fighting, a samurai has to have peace of mind. In a sense, it is giving the word peace a different meaning. You can have action and nonaction, but not peace.

Robert Fisk

I used to play the violin, so I like music very much. I read history books, I travel a lot. I don't look for solace. Why should I want solace? I read because I am interested in history. I swim sometimes. I used to play tennis a lot. I am normal; I go on the Tube and travel on airplanes, and read newspapers; I enjoy fine champagne and I listen to music.

Seyyed Hossein Nasr

I find my peace within by living with God within. It is as simple as that. It comes from leaving everything in God's hands. I have followed Sufism since I was a young man, and the practice of

Sufism involves being able to live in the proximity of the divine reality within us. There is a saying of the Prophet of Islam, "The heart of the believer is the throne of the divine compassionate." The important thing is to reach that heart. We cannot attain inner peace at the psychological level of the world in which we spend most of our time, where we swim in this world of tensions and contentions. We can only find peace by penetrating into our hearts where the divine resides.

"We can only find peace by penetrating into our hearts where the divine resides."

SEYYED HOSSEIN NASR

Harry Dean Stanton

I don't find that peace happens when people have the same common fear, the fear of death, which is fear of nothing. To get to the point where you can face this void, this nothing before you die, I think is a state of enlightenment. To surrender to God is peace and bliss and no fear. God is everything so if you are one with God, you are God. That is what Christ would say, that's what the Buddha said—everything is joined, everything is one.

Sophia Loren

I am most at peace when I am thinking of my sons and of their future.

Anjelica Huston

I try to dance out my anxieties. I like to be near the water. I like to laugh and be with my family and friends. I like to think I have done something good, a little good every day, even if it's thanking someone for a service rendered, small acts of kindness. Nature, green grass, animals, nature again, are very important to me. And true love, people you surround yourself with.

Shimon Peres

I find peace by trying to control my own character, which is not perfect, and by understanding that nothing in life is simple or easy or free. I don't lose heart when I see difficulties; I think it is part of the story. I know that everything important in life takes time, nothing falls from heaven. When I am in a terrible mood, I remind myself that you have to forgive other people as much as yourself, and, as one forgives oneself so much, one should be a little generous about other people as well.

Gianfranco Ferre

When I have been able to achieve what I have wanted to in order to express what I have in my mind and in my heart, that is the major thing that makes me peaceful.

"I find inner peace by drowning out the noise."

BONO

Jack Nicholson

When you have true inner peace, you are probably unaware of it. Real peace is unselfconscious. This can occur when you pull back from the frenzy and retire. I like my job, the acting part of my work, because it can make people think about life. You feel in a small, incremental way you are doing good work. So I think it's also possible, and desirable, to be peaceful while active.

David Frost

Well, I don't seek peace, in the sense of feeling that I haven't got it. People often ask me what I do to relax. I say I'm not tense, I don't need to relax, I enjoy what I do, and I think that is part of it. I don't ever feel I have to go and seek peace of mind. It comes with living up to your principles, I suppose. We are all imperfect, and do not fulfill everything that we set out to do. If, broadly speaking, you are living according to your principles, then I think peace of mind is part of the deal.

Richard Dawkins

I find peace in human contact, friendship, and love. In music. And, indeed, in understanding. One of the supreme joys of life is to be privileged to understand, and science gives me that privilege.

David Lynch

I have meditated for 28 years, so transcendental meditation is how I find my peace.

"Feeling one's soul, silent and still. Knowing I can always return to that place."

MICHAEL FITZPATRICK

Michael Fitzpatrick

The most peaceful place I know is on the stage, playing my cello. When the music is coursing through you, it takes you through "levels" of peace, each one more sublime, more rapturous. Time is suspended and you float on an endless sea of sound. When I am not on stage, being in nature brings me great peace. Something about hearing the sounds of the natural world, of time slowing down, of receiving. Meditating in the stillness and the silence. Being in the trees. Watching the water. Drinking the sunshine in through the eyes, feeling the golden glow and warmth of the sun. Feeling one's soul, silent and still. Knowing I can always return to that place.

Alfredo Guevara

Reading, solitude, and meditation bring me peace.

Dadi Janki with Sister Jayanti

The power of good karma, based on truth, allows peace to stay within me. If you do good works for others, then you will receive peace yourself. What causes sorrow is collecting turmoil from outside you and gathering it in. It is a lack of wisdom to exaggerate little things and allow them to become big.

Ilana Goor

I never find peace because I feel there is no such thing. The minute you find peace, it means you are dying. I am always busy, going from one project to another. A project is never peace, it is excitement. When I don't have a project I'm sick, so it's really not peace, and then when I finish something and look at it, it takes awhile until I am 100 percent satisfied, because the best judge is time. So you have to look and look many times, and sometimes it's not working out and it's moving away.

As an artist, everything that you do is like a new birth; it's a new growth. That's the way Picasso lived until the age of 92, and he was a child for the whole of his life. I feel all the artists that I know are like young kids, they never age, because they go from one project to the other. So I guess that is my peace, to have a project and to go after it and bring it alive. And when it is over you will want to relax, but then again you are going to look for something else. Because the minute you are not doing something, you are dead. My work is my excitement.

Farah Pahlavi

In general, I am at peace with myself because I believe that the positives outweigh the negatives in life. I transcend negative human behavior by taking refuge in nature, listening to music, reading poetry, and by meditating. My greatest joy is the smile of my children and a hug from my grandchildren.

It is my conviction that in the end light will prevail over darkness.

Gore Vidal

I don't look for peace. That is how I find it. If you look for peace in yourself, you won't find it. I find peace in being me, that's to say generally at war. Sometimes I worry that I am too belligerent, but I am not about to change—I am what I am.

Jools Holland

I've always been able to relax completely, and I sleep alright. I don't think I'm particularly in control of anything, so I just take things as they come. I'm happy to play solo or to thousands of people who pay to listen. It doesn't make any difference. So I've got a good job that I enjoy doing. It's the act of playing rather than the finished record that's important.

Mangosuthu Buthelezi

I find my peace with music, church music, classical music like Mozart, and opera. It is so soothing. My mother was a composer and musician and a very remarkable woman. She was posthumously awarded a National Order, as a present for those who have distinguished themselves in culture and art. I was both happy and sad, because I wish she could have been there and witnessed the recognition herself.

Jilly Cooper

I feel most at peace after a really good day's work. The best moment of all is writing "The End" on the last page of a book. I find comfort in shambling through Gloucestershire with my dogs. The countryside is so beautiful it just breaks your heart. I also find enormous peace in listening to music, reading, looking at paintings, and being with family and friends. As I fall asleep, I like to feel my cat, Rattle, landing on my chest and rubbing his purring, furry, black-and-white face against mine as he falls asleep too. That is peace.

Zac Goldsmith

The truth is I probably don't have a means of finding inner peace. My line of work requires that I remain in touch with the horrors that surround us. Sadly, there is no shortage of them. My work involves addressing on a daily basis the reality that we are facing extinction. And whether it will be through climatic instability, wars, disease, or famine, it will be unpleasant. My work involves observing the death of thousands of beautiful species at the hands of modern industrial society. The only peace in my work is the knowledge that I am working on these issues. Outside of this, I try to balance my life through building a farm, growing my own food, planting trees and gardens, rejuvenating local streams and river systems, and raising children of my own within an inspiring family.

Ed Begley Jr.

I make up a gratitude list, and find a lot of solace in that. I really don't want for much. I have my health, my beautiful daughter, my wife, my grown children, so many wonderful friends; I don't think you get any richer than that. I have other tools that I use to achieve peace. I ride my bicycle every day up over the hill over Mulholland from the valley side and I go down to the lake, and that's as high as I ever wanted to be. It's kind of a metaphor for my life. There are hills that you need to scale, psychological ones, physical ones, and coming down the other side you get a rush that's well worth the climb.

Basically, we all cherish tranquillity. For example, when spring comes, the days grow longer, there is more sunshine, the grass and trees come alive and everything is fresh. People feel happy. In autumn, one leaf falls, then another, then all the beautiful flowers die until we are surrounded by bare, naked plants. We do not feel so joyful. Why is this? Because deep down, we desire constructive, fruitful growth and dislike things collapsing, dying, or being destroyed. Every destructive action goes against our basic nature: building, being constructive, is the human way.

To pursue growth properly, we need to renew our commitment to human values in many fields. Political life, of course, requires an ethical foundation, but science and religion as well should be pursued from a moral basis. Without it, scientists cannot distinguish between beneficial technologies and those which are merely expedient.

Unless our minds are stable and calm, no matter how comfortable our physical condition may be, they will give us no pleasure. Therefore, the key to a happy life, now and in the future, is to develop a happy mind.

ABOUT THE CONTRIBUTORS

Ed Begley Jr.

Actor

Ed Begley Jr. has received six Emmy nominations for the TV series *St. Elsewhere* (1982–1988). Involved in environmental affairs, in 1993 he was named Environmental Affairs Commissioner for the City of Los Angeles. He has also worked for the Santa Monica Mountains Conservancy.

Frei Betto

Dominican friar, writer, and leading developer of liberation theology

Published in several languages, Betto was imprisoned from 1969 to 1973 during the military dictatorship in Brazil. He has been chosen as Intellectual of the Year by the Brazilian Writers Union and won the literary Jubuti Award. An advisor to President "Lula" da Silva, he helped plan the "Zero Hunger" antihunger program launched in 2003.

Countess Albina Du Boisrouvray

Philanthropist, president, and founder of the François-Xavier Bagnoud Association and Foundation (AFXB)

Albina is known worldwide for her work on behalf of children's rights. In 1989, following the death of her son, François-Xavier Bagnoud, a helicopter rescue pilot who was killed while on a mission, she set up AFXB. The organization has initiated innovative projects in 17 countries around the world to help children who are victims of AIDS. Under her guidance, AFXB launched

World AIDS Orphans Day, now observed globally on May 7 every year. Albina has received many awards citing her passion and commitment to social and economic development and human rights.

Bono

Musician, lead singer of the band U2, debt campaigner, and activist

Bono has involved himself in many projects and causes including the cancellation of Third World debt, AIDS awareness in Africa, and the Make Poverty History campaign. He has been nominated for the Nobel Peace Prize, made a Chevalier de l'Ordre National de la Légion d'Honneur (2003), and named *Time* magazine European of the Year (2004).

Prince Mangosuthu Buthelezi

President of the Inkatha Freedom Party since it was founded in 1975

Chairman of the House of Traditional Leaders in South Africa's KwaZulu Natal province, Buthelezi is a strong proponent of the African humanistic ideology known as *ubuntu*.

Paulo Coelho

Writer

Coelho is the best-selling author of *The Alchemist* (1988). His latest book is called *The Zahir* (2005). He has collaborated with Brazilian rock musician Raul Seixas on more than 60 songs. His many awards include the Chevalier de l'Ordre National de la Légion d'Honneur (1999).

Jilly Cooper

Author

A journalist and prolific nonfiction writer in her native UK, Cooper is most widely known for her best-selling novels, several of which have been adapted for television.

His Holiness The 14th Dalai Lama, Tenzin Gyatso

Head of state and spiritual leader of the Tibetan people

A number of Western universities and institutions have conferred peace awards and honorary doctorate degrees in recognition of the Dalai Lama's distinguished writings in Buddhist philosophy and for his leadership in the resolution of international conflicts, human-rights issues, and global environmental problems. His Holiness was awarded the Nobel Peace Prize in 1989 in recognition of his nonviolent struggle for the liberation of Tibet.

Professor Richard Dawkins

Charles Simonyi Professor of the Public Understanding of Science, Oxford University

Professor Dawkins has written many books on evolution and science, notably *The Selfish Gene* (1976). Dawkins was awarded an Honorary D.Litt. by the University of St. Andrews (1995) and received the Humanist of the Year award (1996). He is vice-president of the British Humanist Association and a fellow of the Royal Society of Literature.

Charles Le Gai Eaton

Authority on Islam and former consultant to the Islamic Cultural Centre, London

Charles Le Gai Eaton has written several books on religious perspectives, including *Islam and the Destiny of Man* (1976).

Gianfranco Ferre

Designer

Gianfranco Ferre began his fashion career in 1970 and started his own company in 1974. This company, based in Milan, is now one of the world's top fashion houses.

Robert Fisk

Middle East correspondent for the Independent

Robert Fisk has received the British International Journalist of the Year award seven times. In 1990, while serving as *The Times* foreign correspondent in Beirut, he published *Pity the Nation,* describing the war in Lebanon during the 1970s and 1980s. His other awards include Amnesty International UK Press awards (1998 and 2000) and the John Hopkins SIAS-CIBA prize (1996) for international journalism.

Michael Fitzpatrick

Cellist

Recipient of the Prince Charles Award for outstanding musicianship, Fitzpatrick is dedicated to using music as a vehicle for peace, and has worked with the Dalai Lama for the past 10 years on an East-West musical collaboration called *Compassion*.

Sir David Frost

Presenter and interviewer

Sir David Frost has been in the frontline of news and entertainment for nearly 40 years. He has written 15 books, made eight films, and received many major TV awards internationally.

Sir Bob Geldof

Musician, founder of the band the Boomtown Rats, activist, and founder of Live Aid

Geldof has promoted causes including Third World debt cancellation and Make Poverty History. He was awarded an honorary knighthood in 1986 and has been nominated for the Nobel Peace Prize.

Amos Gitai

Filmmaker

Major retrospectives of Gitai's work have been held in Jerusalem, the USA, Frankfurt, London, Paris, and Madrid. He has received several nominations at the Cannes and Venice Film Festivals, and his many awards include the 1989 Venice Festival Critics' Award.

Zac Goldsmith

Environmentalist, director and editor of the Ecologist *since 1998*

As a campaigner on the threats posed by global corporations, Goldsmith has supported the Organic Targets Bill Campaign, among other initiatives. He has contributed to environmental awareness, raising grants of over £5 million in the United Kingdom.

Ilana Goor

Sculptor and designer

Goor's works have been on display in galleries and museums throughout the world since the 1970s. She is also founder of the Ilana Goor Museum in Old Jaffa, Israel.

Robert Graham

Scultptor

Robert Graham is a full member of the National Academy of Design, New York City. He has created numerous public monuments, including the Great Bronze Doors of the Cathedral of Our Lady of the Angels in Los Angeles (2002). He is a Commander in the Knights of Malta.

Alfredo Guevara

President of the Cuban Institute of Cinematographic Art and Industry, ICAIC

Guevara founded the ICAIC shortly after the Cuban Revolution in 1959, eventually retiring from his post as president in 2000. Guevara has also served as the Cuban ambassador to UNESCO.

Jools Holland

Musician and presenter

Holland has performed and recorded with some of the world's most talented musicians. In 2003, he received an OBE for services to the British music industry.

Anjelica Huston

Actress and director

In 1986, Huston won an Oscar as Best Supporting Actress for her role in the film *Prizzi's Honor.* She has earned additional Academy Award nominations for *Enemies: A Love Story* in 1990 and *The Grifters* in 1991.

Dadi Janki

Joint Administrative Head of the Brahma Kumaris World Spiritual University

In 1937, at the age of 21, Janki joined the Brahma Kumaris and soon became one of India's first female leaders, gaining further prominence when the Brahma Kumaris were given affiliation at the United Nations as a nongovernmental organization. She is also founder president of the Janki Foundation for Global Healthcare and vice-president of the World Congress of Faiths.

The Reverend Dr. Una M. Kroll

A long-term advocate of women's ordination to the priesthood, in 1977 Kroll became the first woman to be ordained as a priest in the Church of Wales.

Sophia Loren

Actress

Among her many awards, Loren was the first performer to win an Oscar for a foreign-language film *(Two Women),* in 1961, and was also voted best actress the same year at the Cannes Film Festival.

DAVID LYNCH

Director, writer, and producer

Lynch won the Golden Palm for Best Director at the Cannes Film Festival for *Wild at Heart* in 1990. He has also been nominated three times at the Academy Awards for best director (*The Elephant Man* [1986], *Blue Velvet* [1980], and *Mulholland Drive* [2001]).

NELSON MANDELA

The first democratically elected State President of South Africa

As a lawyer, Mandela held various positions within the African National Congress before being sentenced to life imprisonment in 1962. Released in 1990, he was elected President of the ANC in 1991 and (along with F. W. de Klerk) was awarded the Nobel Peace Prize. In 1994, he was elected State President of South Africa, serving until 1999. He continues to campaign for human rights and the eradication of poverty.

SEYYED HOSSEIN NASR

Professor

Nasr serves as Professor of Islamic Studies at George Washington University, Washington D.C., and President of the Foundation for Traditional Studies, and is the author of many books on Islam.

Jack Nicholson

Actor, writer, and director

Nicholson has won several awards, including Best Actor Oscars for *One Flew Over the Cuckoo's Nest* (1975) and *As Good as It Gets* (1997).

Her Imperial Majesty Farah Pahlavi

The Empress of Iran

Farah Pahlavi married His Imperial Majesty Mohammad Reza Shah Pahlavi of Iran in 1959. She was crowned as Empress (Shahbanou), with the title of Her Imperial Majesty in Teheran in 1967. She continued to pursue her interests in social work, women's rights, sports, and art as Shahbanou of Iran. Following the fall of the Shah and the Islamic Revolution in 1979, Pahlavi lives in exile in Egypt, France, and the USA. She has since written her memoir, *An Enduring Love: My Life with the Shah.*

Shimon Peres

Deputy Prime Minister of Israel

Shimon Peres has also held the posts of Prime Minister, Minister of Defense, and Minister of Foreign Affairs. He received the Nobel Peace Prize, jointly with Yitzhak Rabin and Yassir Arafat, for their efforts to create peace in the Middle East in 1994.

Michael Radford

Director and writer

In 1995, Radford directed the Oscar-nominated and award-winning film *Il Postino.*

Emma Sergeant

Artist

Emma Sergeant is well known for her portraits and paintings of mythical subjects. She has been an official artist with HRH the Prince of Wales, and her work is exhibited at the Fine Arts Society, London.

Harry Dean Stanton

Actor

A prolific award-winning character actor, Stanton is also an accomplished musician.

Sharon Stone

Actress

In 1996, Sharon Stone received an Academy Awards nomination as Best Actress for *Casino.* She won a Golden Globe in the same year, and she was nominated in 1993 for *Basic Instinct.*

Sir Peter Ustinov

Actor, writer, and director

Double Oscar-winning actor and Chancellor of Durham University in the UK, Peter Ustinov served as a Goodwill Ambassador for UNICEF from 1968 until his death in 2004.

Steve Vai

Musician

Vai first stepped into the spotlight in 1980 as a guitarist in Frank Zappa's band. In 1998 he cocreated (with Richard Pike) the Make a Noise Foundation, which is dedicated to assisting young musicians.

Gore Vidal

Author

Novelist, playwright, and essayist, and one of the great stylists of contemporary American prose, Vidal has always been active in politics. He wrote his first novel, *Williwaw,* at the age of 19 in 1946.

Author's Acknowledgments

I would like to thank everyone who supported me during the writing of this book.